Energy Issues and Alliance Relationships:

**The United States,
Western Europe and Japan**

Robert L. Pfaltzgraff, Jr.

Special Report
April 1980

INSTITUTE FOR FOREIGN POLICY ANALYSIS, INC.
Cambridge, Massachusetts, and Washington, D.C.

Requests for copies of IFPA Special Reports should be addressed to the Circulation Manager, Special Reports, Institute for Foreign Policy Analysis, Central Plaza Building, Tenth Floor, 675 Massachusetts Avenue, Cambridge, Massachusetts 02139. (Telephone: 617-492-2116). Please send a check or money order for the correct amount along with your order.

Standing orders for all Special Reports will be accepted by the Circulation Manager. Standing order subscribers will automatically receive all future Special Reports as soon as they are published. Each Report will be accompanied by an invoice.

IFPA also maintains a **mailing list** of individuals and institutions who are notified periodically of new Institute publications. Those desiring to be placed on this list should write to the Circulation Manager, Special Reports, at the above address.

A list of IFPA publications appears on the inside back cover.

The Institute for Foreign Policy Analysis, Inc., incorporated in the Commonwealth of Massachusetts, is a tax-exempt organization under Section 501(c)(3) of the U.S. Internal Revenue Code, and has been granted status as a publicly-supported, nonprivate organization under Section 509(a)(1). Contributions to the Institute are tax-deductible.

Price: $6.50

First Printing
Printed by Corporate Press, Inc., Washington, D.C.

Contents

Preface

This Special Report is the outgrowth of research conducted by the author under the auspices of the International Security Studies Program of the Fletcher School of Law and Diplomacy and the Institute for Foreign Policy Analysis. This research was initiated in the mid-1970s as part of a broader study of the implications of resource scarcity for conflict, including problems arising among members of the alliances that are most vital to the United States. Events subsequent to the October 1973 War and the consequent increases in oil prices, together with the growth in political instability in energy-resource producing states, have served only to give renewed impetus to an understanding of the inextricable link between resources and security. This Special Report is designed to examine the effects of energy issues arising from oil and nuclear power and to assess their implications for alliance relationships and for American policy.

Parts of ongoing research from this project have been presented by the author at conferences held under the auspices of the International Security Studies Program at The Fletcher School of Law and Diplomacy and published in a book produced by the Program entitled *Arms Transfers to the Third World: The Military Buildup in Less Industrial Countries* (Boulder, Colorado: Westview Press, 1978), co-edited by Uri Ra'anan, Robert L. Pfaltzgraff, Jr., and Geoffrey Kemp. Additional publications by the author from this research include "Systèmes d'alliances et problème énergétique dans les annes 80" (*Politique Internationale,* Paris, Summer 1979), and *Instability in Energy Supply: Implications for U.S.-European Relations,* Occasional Papers, Center for International Security Studies, University Center for International Studies, University of Pittsburgh, January 1980. This paper is based upon a presentation by the author at a colloquium held under the auspices of the University Center for International Studies, University of Pittsburgh, in February 1979. Other portions of research conducted on this project have been published in *The Atlantic Community in Crisis: Redefining the Atlantic Relationship* (New York: Pergamon Press, 1979), co-edited by Walter F. Hahn and Robert L. Pfaltzgraff, Jr. A paper containing research from the project was presented at the conference entitled The Future of Nuclear Power, held in Honolulu, Hawaii, between October 31 and November 3, 1979, co-sponsored by the Institute for Foreign Policy Analysis in association with the Industrial Research Institute of Japan, the Konrad Adenauer Foundation of Germany, and the Pacific Forum.

This research was made possible by a grant to the International Security Studies Program of The Fletcher School of Law and Diplomacy by the Rockefeller Foundation and a grant to the Institute for Foreign Policy

Analysis from the Thyssen Foundation in support of current research on resource vulnerabilities confronting the United States and its industrialized allies. Generous support for the Conference on The Future of Nuclear Power was provided by the Konrad Adenauer Foundation. The author benefited from critiques of, and comments on, earlier drafts of the manuscript by Jacquelyn K. Davis, Dr. Daniel Fine, Admiral Robert Hanks (USN, Ret.) and Dr. Charles Perry, of the Institute for Foreign Policy Analysis.

This is the first of several Special Reports to be published by the Institute on security and energy-resource issues. These tentatively include Soviet maritime strategy and the control of chokepoints; Soviet minerals policies; problems of scarcity in strategically important minerals; and a U.S. rapid deployment force.

Robert L. Pfaltzgraff, Jr.

Summary Overview

Energy dependence constitutes the most immediate security threat confronting the United States, Western Europe and Japan in the 1980s. If the experience of the 1970s is illustrative, energy issues introduce into Alliance relationships interests which may be deeply divisive for states with otherwise convergent interests or policy perspectives. The short-term needs of states most heavily dependent on imports of energy are likely to lead to national, rather than collaborative multilateral, efforts by Alliance members to achieve stability of supply. This was the immediate response of industrialized energy-importing states to the Middle East War of October 1973 and the fourfold increase in energy prices in 1973-1974. However, the United States and its industrialized allies took steps, including the formation of the International Energy Agency (IEA), to provide a multilateral framework for the resolution of longer-term issues of energy supply and demand.

Major Energy Issues for the 1980s

In the mid-1970s, Western Europe and Japan, to a greater extent than the United States, confronted several major policy issues and dilemmas. These related to how to assure stability of supply in light of OPEC production cutbacks; how to respond to a selective embargo against states, in particular the Netherlands; how to cope with the problem of sharply increasing oil prices; and how to relate immediate national concerns— i.e., the need to minimize economic dislocations—with broader interests both within the European Community and among Western Europe, the United States and Japan. Whatever the dislocations resulting from the events of the early- to mid-1970s, the problems confronting the United States and its industrialized, energy-consuming states in the 1980s result from the convergence of three major forces which, projected into the decade ahead, yield ominous implications for the United States and its industrialized allies:

(1) The potential for further political instability within Middle East-Persian Gulf oil-producing states, and perhaps on an even broader level, will pose a grave danger to energy supplies. It is apparent that the potential for political instability in the Persian Gulf itself, beyond the Iranian revolution, is enormous. Even in the absence of domestic unrest, the Saudi leadership is likely to face increasing pressure from external sources of instability and conflict. The removal of Iran as a stabilizing influence in the Persian Gulf will give impetus to incipient rivalries within and among states in the region. Saudi Arabia probably will be called upon to play a larger regional security role, particularly with respect to the air and sea

lines of communication along the Persian Gulf and the Red Sea. If the impetus for such a regional role for Saudi Arabia increases, so will the problems created by the country's growing vulnerability to revolutionary forces.

(2) Even in the absence of political instability, economic factors alone might be sufficient to produce energy shortages or at least an uncertain relationship between energy supply and demand. The petroleum available to consuming states in the early- to mid-1980s will come from reserves which have already been identified. It has been estimated that in order to keep pace with world demand for oil in the next decade it would be necessary to have discovered another North Sea- or Alaskan-size oil deposit every three years in the 1970s, since it takes at least a decade to bring new oil discoveries into production. If the various projections about energy supply-demand relationships are compared, what emerges is a substantial level of consensus about the conditions that will face the United States and other energy import-dependent states in the 1980s. Projections completed in the 1974-1975 period generally concluded that declining economic growth rates would result in lower rates of increase in energy consumption and energy demand elasticity, producing a gradual decline in energy imports. In more recent studies there has been an upward revision in projections for net oil imports because of greater reductions forecast in indigenous supplies than had been envisaged—which does not augur well for efforts to reduce drastically our imports of oil in the years just ahead.

(3) The question of oil supply and demand is made more complex as a result of consumption and projection trends in the Soviet Union. By the mid-1980s, the Soviet Union may have become a net importer of oil. Even if a decision were to be made now to develop vast Soviet Siberian oil and natural gas reserves, the lead-time would be so great that the decision would have little effect on Soviet demand for energy imports in the next decade. Such a policy decision, requiring large-scale exports of American technology, would have ramifications beyond energy itself. Therefore, we face the prospect that the Soviet Union and the East European communist states, which have been themselves dependent upon Soviet energy imports, will enter the world market. The interruption in Iran of oil exports has already led East European states to search for alternative sources of oil and natural gas. These trends coincide with an increased or at least a continuing high level of dependence by the United States, Western Europe and Japan upon oil imports and, in particular, imports from the Persian Gulf.

Energy and International Security

The capacity of the Soviet Union for the global projection of naval power and other military capabilities is increasing at a time when that of the United States has declined and the dependence of industrialized, noncommunist states upon sea lines of communication is growing. Moscow sees its interests served by exploitation of rising hostility among Third World states to the industrialized West and to the United States in particular; and by the replacement, where possible, of regimes whose nationalism has proven an obstacle to Soviet control by regimes directly linked to Moscow, as a means of acquiring bases for the projection of Soviet military power. This changed Soviet tactic, generally unnoticed in the Western world, has been evident in Moscow's efforts to replace less pro-Soviet regimes with more pro-Soviet ones.

Given its massive military buildup and its increasing ability to project power abroad, the Soviet Union is attaining a position of unprecedented military power in its strategic relationship with the United States. This will enable the Soviet Union to play an increasingly active role in energy issues of vital importance to the United States and its allies. This must be prudently assumed to be the motivation for a clearly evident drive for hegemony in the Persian Gulf region.

Thus, resource issues have contributed to the need for a conception of security which encompasses geostrategic problems such as the protection of resources located in regions outside the North Atlantic area as well as the waterways through which these resources must pass from producer states to consumer countries. The problem confronting the United States and its industrial allies in energy supply in the 1980s differs in several important respects from the 1973-1974 period. The immediate difficulty is that of assuring the flow of oil and perhaps other strategically important resources from producer countries in a region characterized by growing political instability. In the short term, the threat of massive energy disruption resulting from political instability in the Persian Gulf may call for solutions that are essentially military in nature as the alternative to "economic strangulation," especially if such disruptions come at a time when the stockpiles of oil in the United States, Western Europe and Japan have already been depleted.

Several contingencies can be postulated in which the use of military power can become necessary. These include attacks against tankers by naval forces and aircraft operating in the Persian Gulf; destruction of such shipping by the laying of mines; closure of the Strait of Hormuz; and attacks against ships with weapons launched by units operating ashore.

A revolutionary change in one or more producer states, and especially in Saudi Arabia—as a result of which production ceased or slowed greatly—represents another contingency in which the use of force would become the most prominent option. These contingencies are by no means mutually exclusive; combinations of them could occur simultaneously. The problems inherent in the use of military force increase in complexity, difficulty and uncertainty, from the first to the last contingency. Yet another contingency, the product of the hostage crisis in Iran, is the utilization of military power to *prevent* the export of oil, to cut off other trade, and to rescue American hostages.

The use of force represents an option for which the United States must seek to develop a more adequate capability for the projection of military power. Events of the 1978-1980 period have demonstrated amply the deficiencies of American capabilities in projecting military power to the Persian Gulf, or to adjacent regions, and consequently the need for substantially greater emphasis in the early 1980s on the development of a rapid deployment force and the acquisition of military facilities in Oman, Kenya, Somalia and elsewhere in the region. Such capabilities should include the permanent stationing of a carrier naval task force in the Indian Ocean, together with the development of a rapid intervention force perhaps encompassing the use of airlift for the U.S. Marine Corps.

Nuclear Energy: An Alternative

In addition to oil, nuclear power provides an issue with potential for discord between the United States and its industrialized allies. Although nuclear power does not offer across the board a substitute for petroleum for the remainder of this century, a substantial portion of world energy needs, especially electricity, can and must be met by this energy source. The paradox, if not the internal logical inconsistency, of U.S. nuclear energy policy stems from, on the one hand, placing emphasis on energy shortage forecasts for the mid-to-late 1980s while, on the other hand, restricting severely or postponing the development of more promising new sources of energy. In light of impending energy shortages, nuclear power is becoming indispensable as a substitute for fossil fuels, especially oil. Reactor technology offers the prospect of providing an additional source of energy in the 1990s and the early decades of the twenty-first century in an era between the decline in petroleum resources relative to energy needs and the emergence of new forms of abundant energy.

In the early 1970s, some non-nuclear weapons industrialized states had shown a substantial increase in interest in uranium enrichment, and several West European states had begun to develop their own reprocessing facilities. By the mid-1970s, however, the United States had objected strenuously to proposed exports of German and French nuclear reactors and fuel cycle technology to Third World states—especially the West German-Brazil Agreement of 1975. In October 1976, President Ford had placed restrictions of the sale of new processed nuclear fuel; and under the Carter Administration, the issues that divide the United States and its industrialized allies on nuclear power were sharpened as the United States sought to tighten controls on the use by other states of uranium supplied by the United States. Furthermore, industrialized allies of the United States, especially France, have seen the need to develop nuclear power as rapidly as feasible as a means of diversifying energy supplies. This includes the building of the breeder reactor. The official U.S. position has been based upon the assumption, with respect to the breeder reactor, that the potential risks of proliferation outweigh the political gains in energy development, as well as the view that uranium supply is likely to remain abundant at least until the early years of the twenty-first century. Because it is self-sufficient in uranium, the United States enjoys an advantage not available to Western Europe, which contains no indigenous uranium supplies. In a period of constricting uranium availability, the United States, it is feared, could place additional restrictions on exports to Western Europe and Japan.

In the early 1970s, and especially in the immediate aftermath of the October 1973 War and the energy crisis that ensued, the United States and its industrialized allies placed high hope in nuclear power as an alternative to fossil fuels. By 1979 the United States had in operation 71 nuclear power plants, with about 90 additional plants either under construction or with the necessary permits. Even if every one of the additional 40 plants now on order were to be completed on schedule, the operating nuclear capacity available to the United States by the early 1990s would be only about one-half of what had been projected officially in 1973. The plants under construction at the time of the Three Mile Island accident in 1979, but whose completion may be delayed or canceled, represent the potential equivalent of about 2,000,000 barrels of oil a day. In short, by a combination of policies and as a result of uncertainties, we have effectively lost at least several years in the development of nuclear power as an alternative energy source.

Critical Choices and Alliance Relationships

No single alternative to oil exists and for a large number of users there will be no adequate substitute in the next generation. Nevertheless, the development of nuclear power, together with other approaches to the energy problem, including conservation, would hold promise of having a substantial impact on energy supply over the next generation. Nuclear power represents one of several sources of energy that can, and should, be used. It is essential to evaluate nuclear power as an energy source in the context of consideration of what resources will be available to the United States and other energy import-dependent states, together with their comparative advantages and disadvantages.

The United States and its industrialized, energy import-dependent allies face a series of critical choices with potentially profound effects upon Alliance relationships. The security of the United States and its allies encompasses a series of issues that must be viewed in terms far broader than traditional conceptions of security. They extend not only beyond the geographic confines of the Atlantic Alliance, but also include the role and limitations of force, as well as the political and economic power that inhere in energy and other resources in the late twentieth century. Solutions to such problems, in the short run, are likely to be found in actions taken unilaterally by consuming states most severely affected by disruption in energy supply. Moreover, the shorter the time available to find alternatives to heavy dependence upon oil imports, the greater will be the need for the United States and its allies to consider the use of force in contingencies such as those outlined in this Special Report. This argues for a multi-dimensional policy framework designed to minimize the need for short-term solutions by achieving as quickly as possible, in the next decade, a diversification of energy supply that makes use of each of the most promising alternatives that are likely to be available.

I. An Era of Energy Scarcity

Within the last decade the world has entered an era of resource scarcity, of which the problems of energy furnish the most dramatic and important example. The October 1973 Arab-Israeli War and the temporary interruption of energy supply, together with the fourfold increase in oil prices that followed, symbolized the beginning of this new era. But the events of 1973-1974 were only symptomatic—rather than causal factors in themselves—of the transition to energy scarcity. The meaning of the term energy scarcity itself is fraught with great controversy and ambiguity. The events of the mid-to-late 1970s served to obfuscate, rather than to clarify, its meaning.

The industrialized countries, including the United States, experienced a halting and limited economic recovery from the recession—the worst since the Great Depression of the 1930s—that gripped them in 1973-1975. The exploitation of North Sea oil and Alaskan oil gave to Britain and, to a much lesser extent, the United States a reprieve in which to begin to develop alternatives to existing energy sources and to find new deposits of oil. Despite the increase in the price of oil and the economic recession, however, the United States, by the end of the decade, was far more dependent upon imports of oil, especially from the Middle East, than at the beginning of the 1970s, or even in 1973-1974. Until the revolution in Iran in 1978-1979, oil was once again abundant in the mid-to-late 1970s but at a higher price. However, industrialized states had become dangerously vulnerable to supply interruptions.

As a result, the United States, together with other energy consumers, has perhaps at most a generation, and probably even less time, in which to alter on a massive scale its energy sources. This study examines the events that have led to the energy problems confronting the United States in the late twentieth century, with special emphasis on the numerous linkages among energy issues, alliance relationships and national security.

In the broadest sense, all energy issues have implications for relationships between the United States and its allies in Western Europe and Japan, since they constitute the leading industrial powers and energy-importing states. The focus here is upon those energy issues that seem most likely to affect relations among industrialized states (the United States, Western Europe and Japan) in the last two decades of this century. These are oil and nuclear power—the former because of likely interruptions and shortfalls, and the latter stemming from disagreement about the economic and political costs versus gains, the pace at which development should proceed, and the implications for other issues, such as weapons proliferation, inherent in nuclear energy.

There is an even more important rationale for focusing in this analysis on nuclear energy: It constitutes the principal source that could lessen substantially the dependence of consumer states on oil in the next 10-20 years. All other known alternatives—shale oil, tar sands, solar, wind and ocean waves—would become feasible only if technological breakthroughs are registered. Given the lead-times needed for the development of fusion, which holds promise of eventually providing boundless energy, this source is not likely to become technically feasible at least until the first decades of the 21st century. Hence, the overarching question confronting the leading energy consuming states—the United States and its principal allies—is how they, individually and collectively, will utilize whatever time is available to them in the crucially important and difficult years ahead to provide energy supplies adequate to their needs.

Energy Scarcity and Alliance Relationships

Energy affects relationships among consumer states, especially the United States and its alliance partners in Western Europe and Japan, by virtue of their varying levels of import dependence and divergent approaches to the energy supply problem. The result is to make those states most heavily dependent on imports more vulnerable to interruptions of supply and increases in prices by resource-exporting states and their cartels. Energy issues introduce into alliance relationships interests which may be deeply divisive for states with otherwise convergent interests and policy perspectives, since the short-term needs of those states most heavily dependent upon imports of energy are likely to lead to strictly national decisions, as opposed to multilateral efforts among alliance members, to achieve stability of supply.

Energy issues can stimulate division or cohesion in alliance relationships. In this context, the October 1973 Arab-Israeli War, for example, demonstrated how energy supply problems contribute to divisiveness. The immediate effect of the October War and its aftermath—the temporary interruption in energy supply and the fourfold increase in oil prices—was to produce deep divisions in the Atlantic Alliance, perhaps even surpassing those resulting from the Suez Crisis of 1956.

The October War was notable in Alliance relationships for another reason. It altered the role ascribed to Western Europe and Japan by U.S. foreign policy as emerging power centers in the world of the early 1970s. The

2

concept of a "multipolar" world consisting of a series of power centers, including Western Europe and Japan, was shattered. Western Europe, whose claim to full participation in the global structure conceptualized by American policymakers in the early 1970s rested upon economic strength and growing political unity, was shown to be fragile, not the least because the crisis occurred at a time when the difficult and complex process of building the European Community was subject to reversal and regression. The institutions of the European Community, already weak, seemed further enfeebled in the immediate aftermath of the October War.[1] However, the October War eventually provided stimulus for cooperative European and/or European-Japanese approaches to some issues, including energy, as discussed elsewhere in this Report.

With respect to the energy issues of the 1970s, Western Europe and Japan were shown to be at the mercy of international economic and political forces over which they had little or no control. For a time, Arab oil-producing states exercised unprecedented political influence over Western Europe and Japan. The "oil weapon" was used by producer states to insure that consumer countries adopted policies supportive of the Arab position on Middle East issues. Even so, the European Community, as noted subsequently, advanced policies designed to establish its identity in opposition to U.S. Middle East policy, and the industrialized, oil-consuming states produced a series of frameworks and other arrangements for collaboration.

Aside from highlighting the overall potential for discord, the resource issues that arose out of the October War affected Alliance relations in several more specific ways. These may be grouped in economic-political and strategic-military categories, although there are numerous linkages within and between such categories:

Economic-Political

(1) Inflation generated by rising energy prices placed increased economic constraints upon appropriations for defense. Such inflation, over which import-dependent states had little or no control, was externally or internationally generated.

(2) Balance of payments problems resulting from vastly increased oil import bills gave impetus to the drive for exports, including a perceived need to export larger quantities of arms to the Third World and especially to oil-producing states, thereby stimulating greater competition among alliance members in arms transfers.

---

[1]See Romano Prodi and Albert Clo, "Europe," in Raymond Vernon, editor, *The Oil Crisis* (New York: W. W. Norton, 1976), p. 91.

(3) In the case of the United States, the substantial growth in oil imports by 1977 had contributed to massive balance of payments deficits and a weakening of international confidence in the U.S. dollar. This, in turn, placed severe pressure on the dollar in foreign exchange markets, especially in the late 1970s. The decline in the value of the dollar, relative to other currencies, held important potential implications for the pricing of oil, which has been based on the U.S. dollar.

(4) Large-scale U.S. balance of payments deficits had the effect of increasing international liquidity because of the reserve currency role of the dollar, since such deficits, in effect, "exported" dollars from the United States. This, in turn, increased inflationary pressures in the world economy.

(5) The growth of massive balance-of-payments problems in the United States heightened domestic pressures toward protectionism, thus increasing the potential for discord on trade and monetary policies between the United States and other major industrialized states. Moreover, discord among allies has been increased by the efforts of governments experiencing payments problems (United States) to encourage those in payments equilibrium or surplus (Federal Republic of Germany, Japan) to adopt expansionary domestic economic policies, which such countries, and especially the Federal Republic of Germany, have resisted.[2]

(6) Huge oil import bills contributing to balance-of-payments deficits for some alliance members (such as the United States), and to the disruption of the international economic system, have led to discord over divergent energy policies. In the 1978-1979 period, for example, the perceived inability or unwillingness of the United States to adopt a national energy policy designed to halt or reverse the rising dependence upon imports of energy had generated considerable dissension between the United States and its principal allies.

(7) The sharp increase in oil prices in the 1970s also gave impetus to a search for energy sources hitherto considered to be economically infeasible, with potential consequences of profound proportions for national energy policies and the export of energy-related technologies. For example, with respect to nuclear power, disagreement among Alliance members over the pace, type, export and control of nuclear reactor technology came to the foreground.

Strategic-Military

(1) The problems of security were heightened by virtue of the increased importance of sea lines of communication for resource-import dependent Alliance members, especially between Europe and Japan, but increasingly the United States.

(2) By the late 1970s and early 1980s the most immediate security threats to NATO and to Japan stemmed not only from the vulnerability of oil supplies to interdiction in transit, but also from the prospect of disruption at their source. This

---

[2]See, for example, Paul Lewis, "U.S. to Enter Talks in Paris on Economy," *New York Times*, February 12, 1978, p. 1.

included the potential for political instability in producing states, together with sabotage to oil fields and ports, as well as the possible blockage of the Strait of Hormuz.

(3) The defense of oil extraction facilities in the North Sea became a concern of the Atlantic Alliance and especially of two of its members, Britain and Norway, as such resources came to be exploited in the 1970s.

The effects of each of these resource issues upon alliances are likely to be manifest in the 1980s. The West's major industrialized powers—the United States, the states of Western Europe, and Japan—face the prospect of continued heavy dependence on imports of oil. Although industrialized states have always been dependent upon imports for some raw materials and resources, they have traditionally had greater control over producers, either by virtue of political hegemony in vitally important Third World regions, or as a result of military capabilities with which they could secure such access. Neither of these conditions is present in the late twentieth century, even though the level of dependence of industrialized states upon resource and raw material imports has grown dramatically. In fact, the decline in the military-political presence of the West, and especially of Western Europe (the British military withdrawal from the Persian Gulf was completed in 1972), coincided with the rise in the dependence of industrialized states upon oil imports, especially from the Middle East, as the share of coal in energy consumption declined. These changes, in turn, occurred in a period of increasing cohesiveness, at least on the issue of oil pricing, among producer states in the early 1970s, after OPEC had been largely ineffectual as a cartel in the first decade of its existence.[3] But the cohesiveness of OPEC was heavily dependent on one dominant supplier—Saudi Arabia—whose influence will be especially crucial in oil pricing in the 1980s, whatever the eventual outcome of political instability in Iran.

The Diffusion of Power to Energy-Rich States

The reasons for the decline in the relative bargaining strength of industrialized states are both numerous and beyond the scope of this study. They relate to the wider "diffusion" of power (economic and military) that characterizes our age, together with the rise of a series of states whose possession of mineral wealth provides greater leverage in their relationships with the industrialized world. On the basis of resource wealth, such states seek modernization—by means of Western industrial techniques—and aspire to a position of influence in their respective regions. Such

---

[3]OPEC was founded in 1960.

states also endeavor to strengthen their economic and military potential, thus providing for the industrialized world lucrative markets for the sale of new technology weapons (including, for example, nuclear reactors and related nuclear fuel cycle technology). Weapons systems of unprecedented destructiveness, greater accuracies, and in some cases of lower unit cost are increasingly available on the world market. Nuclear reactors and nuclear fuel cycle technology have become linked—inextricably in some minds—to the issue of nuclear weapons proliferation, with a host of problems not only for relations among industrialized states as sellers of nuclear fuel cycle technology, but also for purchasing states as potential nuclear weapons possessors.

The growth in the economic (and military) power of oil-producing states has profound consequences both within and among the possessors of such capabilities. There is no consensus among analysts as to their stabilizing versus destabilizing consequences. Within states the military power of the government may be enhanced for purposes of internal security, although *economic* modernization may give rise to demands for more effective *political* participation—whether by other modernizing elements or, especially as in Iran, by more traditional elements opposed to some of the social effects of economic modernization. However, Iran, historically, has managed to resemble a nation only when there was a strong military at the disposal of the leader. This situation goes back to the time of Cyrus the Great. When Khomeini returned to Iran, the first step he took was to decapitate the leadership of the various military services— with particular attention to the army. Moreover, the purpose of the mission of U.S. General Robert E. Huyser was apparently to forestall a military coup, telling the Iranian military commanders that if they attempted such a coup, the United States would cut off further aid. Finally, the Iranian military leadership—having always been subject to decisions from the Shah—was left without direction at this crucial moment. At this point, the military declared "neutrality" and retired to the barracks. Had the Chief of Staff of the Air Force—Khatami—not been killed in a hang-glider accident two years earlier, his charismatic figure would probably have held the armed forces together and the story of the Iranian revolution might have been radically different.

The Global Projection of Soviet Power

The growth of Soviet military power at all levels—strategic and conventional, in land forces and naval capabilities—relative to that of the United States imposes additional constraints on noncommunist industrialized states, including the United States, in the utilization of military power for the protection of vitally important resources. The capacity of the Soviet Union for the global projection of naval power—as well as of other military capabilities—is increasing at a time when that of the United States has declined and the dependence of industrialized noncommunist states upon sea lines of communication is growing.

We may project a "worst case" analysis in which the Soviet Union gains a preferential position in one or more oil-producing states of the Persian Gulf. The Soviet Union has already shown a propensity to intervene, with large-scale arms shipments and substantial Cuban proxy forces, in conflicts in Africa. Soviet intervention in the Horn of Africa, first in Somalia and subsequently on the side of Ethiopia, and the invasion of Afghanistan in December 1979, must be viewed in broader geostrategic terms. From one or more countries, the Soviet Union is striving to gain the means of influencing events in the Middle East, especially in the most important oil-producing state, Saudi Arabia. The accession to power of a revolutionary, pro-Soviet Marxist regime in Afghanistan in April 1978, followed by Soviet efforts to replace one client regime with leadership even more fully identified with Moscow, strengthened greatly the position of the Soviet Union in what Zbigniew Brzezinski has termed the "arc of crisis" extending from Southeast Asia to Southern Africa. A Soviet strategy designed to exploit and exacerbate "contradictions" in the noncommunist industrialized world resulting from the energy shortage benefits considerably from the growth of Moscow's influence in the Horn of Africa by virtue of its proximity to Saudi Arabia, and also from the pressure exerted by Soviet-aligned South Yemen against Oman with its geostrategically pivotal position in control of the Musandam Peninsula, which forms part of the Strait of Hormuz.

The existence of numerous conflicts fraught with potential for violence, especially in the Persian Gulf as well as the Horn of Africa and Southern Africa, may provide an irresistible temptation to the Soviet Union. Moscow sees its interests served by exploitation of rising hostility among Third World states to the industrialized West and to the United States in particular; and by the replacement, where possible, of regimes whose nationalism has proven an obstacle to Soviet control by regimes directly linked to Moscow, as a means of acquiring bases for the projection of Soviet military power. This changed Soviet tactic, generally unnoticed in the Western world, has been evident in Moscow's efforts to replace less pro-Soviet regimes with more pro-Soviet ones. It has been attempted, with mixed results, in Afghanistan, South Yemen, Iraq and Ethiopia—all of which are of vital geostrategic importance to the Persian Gulf and the oil supplies of the United States and its industrialized allies.[4]

Although Soviet imports of energy and certain other raw materials may grow substantially in the next decade, the industrialized noncommunist world—and increasingly the United States in particular—is far more vulnerable than the Soviet Union to interruptions in supply in a large number of raw materials because (1) the Soviet policy objective is self-sufficiency and (2) the internal lines of communication of the Soviet Union and its alliances lie for the most part over land, even though the Soviet Union increasingly is dependent on sea lanes and ocean resources. Those of the United States and its allies extend over the world's major maritime routes, including sensitive choke points and narrow seas, adjacent to states and regions where the potential for violence is considerable.[5] Hence, the growth of the world's largest *landpower*, the Soviet Union, to a preeminent position as a *seapower* is fraught with danger for the United States, whose ability to project its own power overseas to protect its interests, including access to energy, on the rimlands of Eurasia is uncertain or has become more costly, both in political and in military terms. The United States, with a two-century-long heritage of maritime competence, is being challenged at sea by another state—the Soviet Union—whose military experience is almost exclusively land-oriented.

TABLE 1
Imports of Raw Materials
(percentages)

	Bauxite	Copper	Nickel	Lead	Zinc	Tin	Cobalt	Iron ore	Manga-nese	Chro-mium
U.S.	88	16	61	12	60	75	94	35	100	90
Europe	50	99	90	85	74	90	98	85	99	95
Japan	100	93	95	78	63	90	98	99	90	95

Source: CIA, *Handbook of Economic Statistics*, ER 77-10537, September 1977, p.17.

[4]For an excellent discussion of this changed Soviet approach to the Third World, see Francis Fukuyama, "A New Soviet Strategy," *Commentary*, October 1979, pp. 52-58.
[5]For an excellent geopolitical analysis of geographic asymmetries between the United States and the Soviet Union, see Colin S. Gray, *The Geopolitics of the Nuclear Era: Heartland, Rimlands, and the Technological Revolution* (New York: Crane, Russak, for the National Strategy Information Center, 1977).

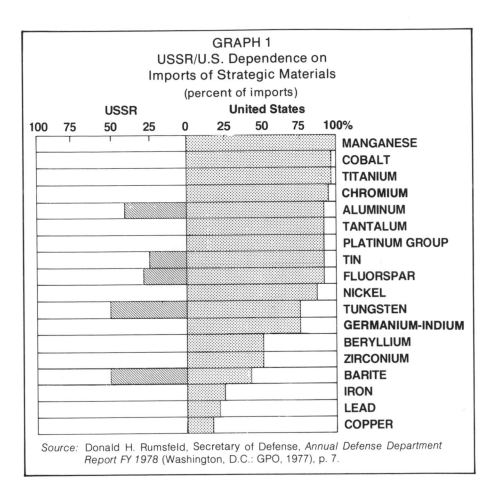

GRAPH 1
USSR/U.S. Dependence on
Imports of Strategic Materials
(percent of imports)

USSR				United States				
100	75	50	25	0	25	50	75	100%

MANGANESE
COBALT
TITANIUM
CHROMIUM
ALUMINUM
TANTALUM
PLATINUM GROUP
TIN
FLUORSPAR
NICKEL
TUNGSTEN
GERMANIUM-INDIUM
BERYLLIUM
ZIRCONIUM
BARITE
IRON
LEAD
COPPER

Source: Donald H. Rumsfeld, Secretary of Defense, *Annual Defense Department Report FY 1978* (Washington, D.C.: GPO, 1977), p. 7.

Geopolitical Factors and Energy Issues

Thus, the effect of the energy and raw material needs both of industrialized nations and of most Third World states is to give even greater importance to the role of geopolitical factors. Geopolitics explores locational or geographic considerations as they relate to power. The geopolitical importance of location (source) is heavily influenced in the late twentieth century by resources generally and by energy specifically. Such factors impinge on U.S. security interests and alliance relationships at several levels:

(1) Energy issues are contributing to, and are affected by, a diffusion of military and economic power that is unprecedented. The world of the next generation will

MAP 1

Main Oil Movements by Sea 1977

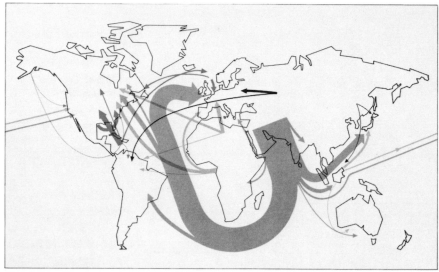

Source: *BP Statistical Review of the World Oil Industry 1977* (London: The British Petroleum Company Limited), p. 15.

probably contain a series of powers whose enhanced status, in some instances at least, will have been attained by wealth from resources and raw materials.

(2) Energy issues and related wealth transfers are contributing not only to the diffusion of advanced non-nuclear defense technologies (weapons of unprecedented accuracy and ease of operation), but also to the prospects for nuclear proliferation by virtue of the greater interest in nuclear energy and the growing export of sensitive nuclear technologies which increase the possibility of developing weapons grade plutonium.

(3) Energy issues are enhancing greatly the importance of the oceans both as a source of food, minerals, and—indeed—energy, as well as for the transit of these vital resources and raw materials to consumer states. The creation of exclusive economic zones (200 miles in the case of several powers, including the United States), and the capability of states, by virtue of new technologies, to extract resources from traditionally hostile maritime environments (e.g., North Sea oil) and to make use of maritime technologies (e.g., supertankers) to move large quantities of resources from point of origin to destination for consumption enhance the importance of the oceans and the seabed. The growing vulnerability of consumer states to the interruption of supply, whether in transit on the oceans or,

perhaps more likely, at its source in the producing state, will have potentially greater consequences for the security of the United States and its allies than for the Soviet Union. Unlike the Soviet Union, the United States and its industrialized allies are linked principally by the seas to the sources of energy upon which they must rely in the 1980s.

(4) The trade deficits confronting some, but not all, oil-importing states have had several important implications—economic and political—for energy import-dependent states and for alliance relationships. In effect, oil-producing countries are lending to oil-consuming states with trade deficits as a result of oil-import bills which are paid by short-term credits. Such credits are concentrated in OPEC states. As a result, the multilateral flow of world trade is said to be reduced, with a multiplier effect through a reduction in demand in some export industries.[6] Here it should be noted that the Federal Republic of Germany and Japan, both far more heavily dependent on oil imports than the United States, have had surpluses in their balance of payments from the mid-to-late 1970s, although by 1980 the Federal Republic had experienced a modest deficit. Hence, however much rising oil imports may have contributed to the massive U.S. payments deficit, the cause lies beyond energy itself.

(5) The inflation that industrialized states faced in the 1970s has defied the efforts of economists to achieve a consensus concerning its causes, remedies and effects. Nevertheless, much of the inflation of the 1970s can be attributed to the fourfold increase in oil prices absorbed by consumer states after 1973, together with further increases by OPEC in June 1979 and subsequently. The sharp rise in oil prices imposed, in effect, a tax upon oil-importing countries, the proceeds of which were transferred to oil-producing states.

In the immediate aftermath of the energy crisis following the October War it was assumed that the huge oil-import bills of oil-consuming states would not be offset by investments and purchases of goods and services by oil-producing states. It was widely held that there would be a transfer of real wealth from oil consumer to producer states, with deflationary effects on the economies of oil-importing states.[7] However, some OPEC countries, by the end of the 1970s, were in payments deficit. Huge OPEC oil revenue surpluses have fallen as oil-producing countries have demonstrated high propensities to purchase imported goods, to invest capital in the diversification of their economies, and to make substantial investments in industrialized oil-consuming states—and as the consuming nations made the first tentative moves toward conservation.

If the generation before 1973 was characterized (as noted later in this study) by a real price decline in oil, so was the period from the mid- to

---

[6]See Guy De Carmoy, *Energy for Europe: Economic and Political Implications* (Washington: American Enterprise Institute for Public Policy, 1977), p. 18.
[7]*Ibid.*, pp. 17-18.

late-1970s, even after the fourfold increase of 1973-1974.[8] Paradoxically, if the increase in oil prices helped to bring on the recession of 1973-1975, the relative decline in the real price of oil contributed to the modest recovery of the mid-to-late 1970s. Between 1975 and 1979 prices of oil increased at a rate below the rate of increase of inflation, in spite of the two 10 percent increases by OPEC in October 1975 and December 1976, followed by a 14.5 percent increase in December 1978. Because the price of oil is calculated in dollars, and because the dollar has depreciated relative to the leading currencies in recent years, there was a further erosion in the real price of oil between January 1977 and April 1978 and a decline in value of more than 22 percent against the Swiss franc and 21.5 percent and 14 percent, respectively, against the Japanese yen and the German mark.[9] The real cost of oil to such countries fell because oil is dollar denominated. Nevertheless, this trend was reversed in 1979, as the scramble for oil in the wake of the Iranian cutbacks led to a dramatic escalation in the cost of crude from several key producers, and to a breakdown in OPEC unanimity on a unified price structure. By the end of December 1979, Saudi Arabia, the United Arab Emirates, Qatar, Kuwait and Venezuela—the so-called "price moderates"—had agreed that the official dollar price for their medium-light crude in 1980 would average between $24 and $27. Official prices among the main African producers—including "price hawks" such as Libya—will cluster around the $33-35 level. Meanwhile, crude supplies on the spot market, which was unusually active in 1979, may continue to sell for as high as $45 a barrel.

International Security

While the advent of new technologies has enhanced the need for resources, as well as the extractive capacity of states (although the latter has not kept pace with the former), it has not given to consuming states a technological capacity for the protection of resources, especially in transit, greater than the destructive potential of other groups, state and nonstate, bent upon interdiction—although this could change eventually as a result of innovations in weaponry. We have entered an era in which weapons of unprecedented accuracy will be more widely available than ever to state and nonstate actors. These include precision-guided, air-

---

[8]As a result, the official OPEC price of "marker" crude, 34° Arab light, was to rise from $12.70 to $14.54. The previous OPEC oil price increases after 1973 included 10 percent to $11.51 in October 1975; an increase of 10 percent by only seven OPEC members on January 1, 1977, with Saudi Arabia and the United Arab Emirates raising their price by only 5 percent, resulting in an official rise of the marker to $12.086 per barrel.

[9]Jahangir Amuzegar, "OPEC and the Dollar Dilemma," *Foreign Affairs*, July 1978, pp. 741-749.

delivered munitions, new artillery munitions, weaponized lasers, surface-to-surface missiles for both maritime and land warfare applications, remotely piloted vehicles, and rocket-propelled grenades. Such weapons will place in the hands of potential users a capability for disrupting technologically advanced societies and, specifically, for interdicting shipping lanes and other transportation routes. Large surface ships, both warships and commercial vessels, will be increasingly vulnerable to precision-guided weapons in the hands of littoral states or other actors[10]—although naval vessels such as the carrier will remain essential to the United States in the projection of military power, especially in the Third World, including the Persian Gulf.

Clearly, resource issues are giving rise to a variety of problems that are of interest to the scholar and to the policymaker in the late twentieth century. They point to the continued and growing importance, as already noted, of geopolitical, or geostrategic, factors in the theory of international relations and as conditioners of foreign policy. They provide evidence of the inherent limits of globalism, regionalism and international organizations in the resolution of "global" issues in an "interdependent" international system. In the energy problems of recent years, we have witnessed what has been termed a growing "politicization"[11] of international economic relations at the state-to-state level and, it might be added, the increased potential for conflict among state and nonstate entities in coming decades as a result of resource issues. Because such issues, especially those related to energy, affect the well-being of noncommunist industrialized countries, whose economies are closely intertwined, they have crucially important implications for relationships between the United States and its principal allies. (The immediate response of West European nations and Japan to the events in Iran—and to those in Afghanistan—possessed a haunting resemblance to Munich. It almost seemed as if these nations believed that by placating the Soviet Union they could appease Moscow's appetite.)

Thus, solutions have been sought, for the most part, by national means rather than through alliances or other multilateral frameworks, even though the relatively greater vulnerability of Western Europe and Japan to interruptions of energy supply holds major implications for the United

---

[10]See Geoffrey Kemp and Robert L. Pfaltzgraff, Jr., "New Technologies and the Emerging Geo-strategic Environment," in Geoffrey Kemp, Robert L. Pfaltzgraff, Jr. and Uri Ra'anan, editors, *The Other Arms Race: New Technologies and Non-Nuclear Conflict* (Lexington, Mass.: D.C. Heath, Lexington Books, 1975), pp. 125-148.

[11]See, for example, Robert J. Lieber, *Oil and the Middle East War: Europe and the Energy Crisis* (Cambridge, Mass.: Center for International Affairs, Harvard University, 1976), p. 53.

States, whose economic well-being would be endangered by the weakening of Western Europe and Japan. The reasons for this predicament will be examined more fully in the next section which assesses trends in energy import dependence of the United States and its principal allies, together with its implications for relations among allies.

2. Energy Dependence and Alliance Relations: The Problem of Oil Supply Security

Import-Dependence Before the October 1973 War

Historically, the United States and most of the states of Western Europe enjoyed access to abundant energy, either within their own national boundaries or as a result of control over overseas sources. West European countries had access to huge reserves of coal within their boundaries—especially in the case of Britain, Belgium and Germany. Oil was available in overseas territories which formed a part of European empires or over which Western Europe held effective economic influence. Indigenous coal was indispensable to the industrialization of Western Europe and the United States. For most of its history the United States was a large exporter of fossil fuels, both coal and oil, although since 1947 the United States has been a net importer of petroleum. By the early 1970s declining U.S. domestic oil production, together with soaring demand, had pushed imports of Arab oil to more than one million barrels per day.[12]

Before World War II, Japan obtained most of her energy from domestically produced hydroelectric power or from coal mines in Manchuria which Japan had seized in 1931. Japan imported oil, principally for her military forces, from the United States and the Dutch East Indies. In July 1941, the United States itself used the "oil weapon" against Japan. The U.S. embargo against oil exports to Japan helped set the stage for the Japanese attack against Pearl Harbor, because Japan concluded that the destruction of American naval power was the indispensable prerequisite to securing oil in Southeast Asia. The occupation of the Dutch East Indies provided an ample source of oil for the Japanese war effort. The Japanese war machine was essentially brought to a grinding halt well before the end of the Second World War because the United States was able to sever the supply line which brought the indispensable oil from Southeast Asia to the home islands of the empire. Although the motivations leading European countries, and later Japan, to seek control over far-flung territories were numerous, the need for resources, and especially oil, formed one important rationale.

---

[12]See James W. McKie, "The United States," in Raymond Vernon, editor, *The Oil Crisis* (New York: W. W. Norton, 1976), p. 73. "Thereafter, total consumption in the United States rose from approximately 6 million barrels per day in 1948 to a bit under 17 million just before the embargo in 1973. Production of domestic crude oil and liquid rose from 5.9 million barrels per day in 1948 to 10.8 million in 1973, but it had peaked in 1970, at 11.2 million. Imports represented over 30 percent of consumption by 1973. . . ."

The end of the imperial dominance of industrialized consumer states was followed by high rates of economic growth with increasing demand for imports of oil no longer under their control. In 1956 Britain and France faced the prospect of an interruption in oil supply as a result of the Anglo-French invasion of the Suez Canal Zone. One of the effects was the growth of interest in European integration, symbolized by the formation of the European Economic Community and the European Atomic Energy Community (Euratom) with the signing of the Rome Treaties in March 1957. By the late 1960s, increasing dependence on Middle East oil had contributed to a growing pro-Arab stance by West European governments. In particular, French policy underwent a dramatic change during De Gaulle's tenure from its earlier pro-Israeli orientation especially at the time of the Six Day War in 1967. Thus, the basis was laid for European discord with the United States because of its commitment to Israel.

The end of the Algerian war in 1962 had made it possible for De Gaulle to seek to re-establish for France a role in the Arab world. De Gaulle set out not only to strengthen France's international position, but also to limit the influence of the "Anglo-Saxon" powers and the Soviet Union and to capture for French industry lucrative arms markets in the Middle East. At the same time France (and Western Europe) was becoming increasingly dependent on Arab oil as most European economies experienced unprecedented growth rates and consumed ever rising amounts of energy. From 1950 to 1970, global production and consumption of energy grew at an average annual rate of 4.2 percent, from 31 million barrels per day in 1950 to 73 million barrels per day of oil equivalent in 1970. Oil and natural gas accounted for virtually all of the growth in production in this period, with the greatest increase occurring in the 1960-1970 decade.[13] At the same time the cost of coal, relative to oil, increased as the wages of miners in this labor-intensive industry rose and as the best layers of coal in Belgium, France and the Netherlands gradually became exhausted.

In the 1960s, there was a 60 percent decline in the number of coal mines in the nine present members of the European Community—from 1.6 million to 615,000.[14] Policies pursued by national governments and by the European Coal and Steel Community resulted in artificially low coal prices below what a market economy would have brought. In penetrating European markets, the oil companies underpriced crude oil and other products which competed directly with coal (being able to do so because

[13]*World Supplies of Primary Energy: 1976-1980* (London: Energy Economics Information Service, Ltd., 1976), p. 1.
[14]Prodi and Clo, "Europe," in Vernon, editor, *op. cit.,* p. 92.

of the artificially low, well-head price of Middle East oil), while over-pricing those products, such as gasoline, for which no indigenous European competition existed. Thus, Europeans were encouraged to abandon coal for oil, and to base their economies on relatively cheap imports of oil.

Between 1960 and 1970, the total imports of energy from outside the European Community grew during each year of the decade even though there were discoveries of oil and natural gas in Europe. These discoveries were especially notable in the early 1970s in the North Sea. By 1972, the production of natural gas in Western Europe totaled 150 billion cubic meters or 95 percent of domestic consumption.[15] During the decade of the 1960s the growth in energy consumption and in energy imports was greater than the growth in energy value related to practically all other goods and services. Western Europe registered sharp increases in living standards, productivity, imports and exports. Energy could be imported at the end of the 1960s for a lower *real* cost than a decade earlier. Despite sharp increases in energy dependence, the share of energy imports in the value of total European Community imports remained relatively stable, with an increase from 14 percent in 1960 to 17 percent in 1970.[16]

In Japan, likewise, oil consumption increased rapidly in the 1960s as a result of soaring economic growth together with the decline in real prices of oil. Between 1960 and 1965 alone, Japan's oil consumption tripled. Oil became the principal energy source in Japan, accounting for 40 percent of primary energy demand in 1960 and increasing to 62 percent by 1965, and more than 70 percent in 1975.[17] In the 1960s, Japan became the largest individual importer of oil. The availability of petroleum—in fact, a glut on the market—made such energy cheaper relative to alternative forms of energy, as well as other basic commodities.

Viewed in broader historical perspective, the period between 1955 and the late 1960s was one of rising energy needs, continuing a trend that had begun just after World War I. This was also a period in which energy efficiency declined, reversing a trend toward greater efficiency of use that had occurred from the end of World War I to the mid-1950s. Between 1918 and 1954, the amount of energy needed to produce a dollar of U.S. Gross National Product, the so-called energy/GNP ratio, had declined

---

[15]*Energy Prospects to 1975*, Vol. 1 (Paris: OECD, 1975), p. 50.
[16]These findings are contained in a study by Resources for the Future, of Washington, D.C.; reported in Anthony J. Parise, "Can We Have our Energy and Burn it Too?," *New York Times*, National Economic Survey, January 8, 1979, pp. 14-16.
[17]*Quarterly Economic Review of Oil in the Far East and Australia* (London: Economist Intelligence Unit, 1977), p. 5.

from a peak of about 92 million BTUs to about 59 million BTUs.[18] This improved efficiency resulted from such innovations as the increased use of electricity in industry and the shift from coal to diesel power in the railroads. The decline in efficiency between 1955 and the late 1960s can be attributed to such phenomena as the growth of large, low-mileage cars, the burgeoning use of appliances such as air conditioners, and lowered rates of efficiency in power plants. In fact, this decline in energy efficiency stemmed in large part from its relative cheapness. In the thirty-year period after World War II, oil became the most important commodity in world trade, and oil companies the most powerful multinational enterprises.[19] The availability of relatively cheap energy, in the form of oil, undoubtedly contributed to the prolonged and unprecedented growth of the world economy in this period.

The increase in energy prices beginning in the early 1970s and accelerating during and after the October War contributed to another reversal in the energy/GNP ratio—to the more efficient use of energy. From a level of just under 58 in 1978, the ratio for the United States is expected to decline to 54.1 in 1980, 52.5 in 1985 and 51.3 in 1990. This would still be higher than the ratio of 41 already achieved in the Federal Republic of Germany and Sweden. The study upon which this analysis is based, by Data Resources, Inc., assumes an average growth rate in U.S. GNP of 3.4 percent a year, with total energy consumption rising by about 2.8 percent a year.[20] Hence, economic growth may be possible without equivalent increases in energy consumption, but this will require conservation measures and more efficient energy use. In fact, economic growth in the 1980s depends upon energy consumption at lower rates of increase than in previous decades, although sharp increases in energy prices resulting in a decline in economic growth rates will reduce the demand for energy and possibly the incentive for efforts to develop new sources of energy as a substitute for oil.[21] However, as petroleum resources continue to

---

[18]According to a European Community study: "Altogether the degree of energy dependence, which expresses in percentage terms the share of supplies originating in countries outside the Community in the total requirements, has grown in the years [between 1960 and 1970] from 39% to 66%, the actual energy imports of the Community rising from 200 million tce (tons coal equivalent) to 650 million tce. The Community thus appears in the first rank of buyers on the world energy market, accounting for approximately 30% of the whole of the world's imports. For crude oil alone, it leads with 406 million tons in 1970, ahead of Japan (142 million tons), EFTA (130 million tons, 94 of which for Great Britain), and the United States (87 million tons)." Commission of the European Communities, *Prospects of Primary Energy Demand in the Community (1950-1980-1985)* (Luxembourg: Office for Official Publications of the European Communities), p. 31.

[19]Mason Willrich, *Energy and World Politics* (New York: The Free Press, 1975), p. 13.

[20]See Parise, *op. cit.*

[21]For an elaboration of this point, see L. G. Broukes, "Energy Policy, The Energy Price Fallacy, and the Role of Nuclear Energy in the U.K.," *Energy Policy*, June 1978, p. 96.

shrink (some will debate this thesis, arguing that plenty remains to be found) competition for those resources will increase, lowered economic growth notwithstanding. Even with lower rates of energy increase than in the late 1970s, the import dependence of industrialized, energy-consuming states will remain substantial in the 1980s.

The October 1973 War and Energy Dependence

The growing West European energy dependence on the Middle East provided both the basis for the dislocation confronting industrialized consumer states during and after the October War and the catalyst for the response of the European Community and its members, Japan, and the United States to the Middle East War, as a result of the curtailment of oil supply and the quadrupling of energy prices. The crisis had two phases, which were related in turn to the shorter-term and longer-term impacts of energy upon Western Europe, Japan and the United States. In the first phase, between October 1973 and February 1974, the problems facing industrialized oil importers stemmed from the curtailment of oil supplies through the embargo against the Netherlands and the United States and the 25 percent reduction in oil production announced by OPEC in October 1973—although it is possible to exaggerate its effects upon Western Europe because of its substantial oil reserves (about a 80-day stockpile[22], together with another 25-day supply in transit to European refineries). The second—and far more serious—problem, which dated from October 1973 and had a multiplicity of dimensions and implications, resulted from the increase in the price of oil.

Specifically, Western Europe and Japan, to a greater extent than the United States, confronted several major policy issues and dilemmas: (1) how to assure stability of supply in light of the OPEC production cutbacks; (2) how to respond to a selective embargo against states, in particular the Netherlands, singled out by the Arab oil producers; (3) how to cope with the problem of sharply increased oil prices (from $2.59 to $11.65 per barrel as posted at Saudi Arabian ports); (4) how to relate immediate national concerns (i.e., the need to minimize economic dislocations) with broader interests both within the European Community and among Western Europe, Canada, the United States and Japan; and (5) how to reconcile relationships among industrialized energy-importing states and oil-producer states. Differences in approach became manifest both within the European Community and in the Atlantic Alliance, and in relations between Japan and the United States.

---

[22]Prodi and Clo, "Europe," in Vernon, editor, *op. cit.*, p. 101.

Although the crisis produced reciprocal recriminations between Japan and the United States concerning the allocation of oil (on the Japanese side, that major oil companies were redirecting oil destined for Japan to supply U.S. needs; on the American side, that the Japanese were helping to bid up the price of oil by making excessive offers in order to secure supplies), Japan, in fact, received one percent more oil during the embargo (January 1–March 31, 1974) than she had during the corresponding period in 1973. This was 11 percent less than the increase in consumption that had been forecasted for Japan, although Japan actually consumed 10 percent more petroleum in the first quarter of 1974 than in the same period a year earlier.[23]

Japan was the only major industrial country to increase its oil consumption during the crisis, although the maintenance of Japan's rate of economic growth depended upon substantially higher imports of oil than were available. Moreover, at the beginning of the crisis, Japan had been classified by the Organization of Arab Petroleum Exporting Countries (OAPEC) as an unfriendly state, thus producing—both in the Japanese government and in the private sector—fear of severe shortages that would reduce industrial output and increase already high rates of inflation. Hence, on November 22, 1973, Japan followed in the wake of the European Community with its own declaration of support for the Arab position with respect to Israel. This Japanese action represented the first time since World War II that Japan had aligned herself in opposition to U.S. policy.

The transatlantic dispute between the United States and its West European allies revolved upon contrasting approaches to the Middle East crisis based on differing levels of dependence on Middle East oil. The perception was widespread that Western Europe faced the specter of economic disaster resulting from the curtailment of energy supplies, although as Romano Prodi and Albert Clo have noted, there was a decrease in consumption in the winter of 1973-1974 that may have been attributable both to the mild weather of that period and the huge increase in oil prices. "In any event, *there was at no time a real shortage* of petroleum on the European market." Consumption simply responded to the increase in prices, thus, incidentally, casting some doubt on the then presumed "rigidity" of petroleum demand. Between October 1973 and April 1974, the reserves of oil products in the countries of the European

---

[23]Robert B. Stobaugh, "The Oil Companies in the Crisis," in *ibid.*, pp. 192-193. See, in the same volume, Yoshi Tsurumi, "Japan," pp. 113-127.

Community never descended below the 80-day equivalent of consumption; and in Italy the reserves in fact increased by 23 percent.[24]

Reciprocal recriminations arose over the lack of consultation on Middle East issues, Western Europe accusing the United States of developing a "condominium" relationship with the Soviet Union, and the United States expressing displeasure with the lack of consultation by the European Community in the formulation of a "European" approach to the Middle East. Widely divergent responses were addressed to the energy crisis, with the United States objecting strenuously to European efforts to conclude bilateral agreements with oil-producing states and the Europeans expressing concern over the lack of American sympathy with the European need to obtain oil wherever possible in order to assure adequate supply. The West Europeans generally favored bilateral agreements (to be discussed later) in an effort to find immediate solutions both to the short-term and longer-term problems of supply and price, respectively. In contrast, the United States embraced multilateral frameworks that, to the Europeans, often appeared inappropriate for the solution of the immediate issues.

These differences represented but the most recent manifestations of issues that had long divided the United States and Western Europe based on divergent and, in some cases, competitive economic relationships, European apprehension that the United States would reach agreements with the Soviet Union without adequate consultation with Western Europe, and evolving European policies which, as noted earlier, have progressively favored the Arab world as Europe's dependence on Middle East oil has grown. The evolution of the European Community, with its cumbersome decision-making structure, has created for European-American relations new problems related as much to the process by which policy is formed as to the substance of policy itself. However, the Middle East crisis of October 1973 brought each of these issues in the transatlantic relationship into sharper focus as Western Europe strove for an "identity" measured, so it seemed, by the divergence of the "European" policy from the United States.

---

[24]Prodi and Clo, "Europe," in *ibid.*, p. 101. (Italics in original.) The authors also suggest (p. 101) that "Between December 1973 and March 1974, the availability of petroleum in the first principal European countries—France, Germany, Great Britain, Italy and the Netherlands—was about 5 percent lower than it had been in the same period a year earlier. Availability was reduced by 16 percent in the Netherlands, 12 percent in Germany, 7 percent in France, not quite 1 percent in Great Britain, and actually increased by about 4 percent in Italy."

In the autumn of 1973, Western Europe's vulnerability to forces over which it had little or no control became more evident than at any time since World War II. Europe was a secondary theater of activity, the object rather than the initiator of vast international forces. Europe faced the prospect of "finlandization" not directly by the Soviet Union but rather by the Arab oil-producing states wielding their new-found oil weapon, against which Europe appeared helpless. The crisis demonstrated the unwillingness, or the temporary inability, of the Europeans to work together to assure adequate supplies of energy to other Community members. In singling out the Netherlands for a total oil embargo, the oil-producing states created for the European Community a challenge, to which the European members, notably Britain and France, responded by agreeing in effect to enforce the oil embargo against the Netherlands.

Yet, within the European Community, there were important differences in approach and in manifestations of hostility to U.S. policy. France adopted a policy far more sympathetic to producer states than did the Federal Republic. French policy was designed not only to assure sustained access to energy but, under the arch-Gaullist Foreign Minister, Michel Jobert, also to establish a "European" policy stance as widely different and divergent as possible and necessary from the United States. Under the Heath Government, which was not without its own Gaullist proclivities, Britain aligned herself with France. At the same time, Britain faced a coal miners' strike, whose immediate effect was far greater than that of the oil crisis, resulting in the fall of the Heath Government in February 1974, as well as the imposition of a three-day work week and other curtailments in coal-produced energy in Britain. The German Federal Republic, torn as almost always between its West European and Atlantic connections, sought to maintain a form of neutrality between Paris and Washington.[25]

In the immediate aftermath of the October War, as postulated in American foreign policy in the early 1970s, perceptions of national interest, of economic nationalism, and of European and Japanese economic interest differing sharply from those of the United States transcended perceptions of transnational interest, of multilateralism and of solidarity in face of challenges posed by producer states.[26] Only after the traumatic events of 1973 did the United States, Western Europe and Japan begin to act in

[25]For a good analysis of French and West German perspectives and policies, see Horst Mendershausen, *Coping with the Oil Crisis: French and German Experiences* (Baltimore, Md.: The Johns Hopkins University Press, 1976), esp. Ch. 4.

[26]The events of late 1973 pointed up the need, however, for the United States and other major noncommunist industrialized states to work more closely together to develop a framework for common action on energy issues. In December 1973, Secretary of State Kissinger had called for the creation of a Trilateral Energy Action Group to strengthen

concert for the resolution of energy issues: in the Washington Energy Conference of February 1974, the formation of the International Energy Agency, and the convening of meetings, including summit conferences addressed to such problems as energy—first in Rambouillet, France, in June 1976, and subsequently in London in May 1977, Bonn in July 1978, Guadaloupe in January 1979, and Tokyo in June 1979.

The Broadened Conception of Alliance Security

The security of Western Europe remains crucially dependent on the preservation of a political-military balance between NATO and the Warsaw Pact. However, the problem of European security, almost from the founding of NATO, has included perceived threats to the Alliance from outside its geographic perimeter. In 1956, the United States opposed British and French military intervention in the Middle East, and earlier in the 1950s Washington was not prepared to give large-scale direct support to France in Southeast Asia. At the time of the Suez Crisis Britain and France faced the prospect of the curtailment of oil supplies. In the 1960s and early 1970s, the West Europeans looked with disdain upon U.S. policies in the Third World, including Southeast Asia and the Middle East. The vulnerability of the industrialized world increased as its dependence on imports of vital resources and raw materials and oil, especially from the Middle East and Persian Gulf, grew. Thus, resource issues have enhanced the need for a geostrategic conception of security that provides for the protection of resources located in regions outside the North Atlantic area, as well as the waterways through which those resources must pass from producer states to consumer countries. The growth of Soviet naval power

---

cooperation among both oil-consuming and oil-producing nations in order to conserve existing energy supplies, develop new resources, and evolve an international collaborative research program for technologies to exploit existing energy sources, such as shale oil, and to find new sources such as solar energy.

From this, together with other initiatives, including the Washington Energy Conference of oil-consuming states (members of the European Community, Norway, Japan and the United States), held in February 1974, came the impetus for the formation of the International Energy Agency established on November 15, 1974, within OECD to develop a program of cooperation in emergencies and for the longer term. The new organization included a Governing Board consisting of ministers or their delegates from member countries, and a Management Committee, composed of senior representatives of each participating country to deal with (a) Emergency Questions, (b) The Oil Market, (c) Long Term Cooperation, and (d) Relations with Producer and Other Consumer Countries. The original twelve members of IEC were Belgium, Canada, Denmark, the German Federal Republic, Ireland, Italy, Japan, Luxembourg, the Netherlands, Norway, United Kingdom and the United States. Austria, Spain, Sweden and Turkey joined in 1975. See *U.S. Energy Policy, October 1973-November 1975, Selected Documents* (Washington, D.C.: Department of State, Bureau of Public Affairs, Office of Media Services, No. 3, December 1975).

relative to that of the United States poses a serious threat to the sea lanes vital to the passage of raw materials and oil in a future crisis.[27]

Energy dependence constitutes the most serious security threat confronting the United States, Western Europe and Japan in the 1980s, and it is prudent to assume that a military conflict between the Warsaw Pact and NATO would be accompanied by action against the Persian Gulf. Thus, contingencies within and outside Europe should not be viewed as mutually exclusive. Yet, industrialized states have been unable, or unwilling, to take steps that would have safeguarded oil supplies located in regions where less than a generation earlier European powers had exercised major influence. The protection of sea lines of communication has fallen increasingly to the United States, even though European powers once maintained an impressive naval presence in, or adjacent to, strategically important waterways. The prevailing mood is to leave to the United States the role of protecting vital sea lines of communication, although military power has not been sufficient in itself to prevent the interruption in oil supply and the rapid increase in the cost of energy.[28]

Whether military power could be usefully employed, in extremis, to seize oil, and under what conditions, at what levels, and with what support among Atlantic Alliance members, are questions that NATO has shown little interest in exploring—although the events of 1978-1980, especially in Iran and Afghanistan, have led to increased discussion, both in the

---

[27]Drew Middleton, "Three Admirals See Soviet Navy Threat," *New York Times*, January 7, 1978, p. 4. According to Admiral Zumwalt: "We simply lack the capability to defend our oil line from the Middle East" and "can't deal with the serious threat to the Atlantic Alliance's flanks." In the event of war with the Soviet Union, "we would abandon our allies in the Western Pacific and concentrate on the defense of Hawaii and Alaska, putting most of our ships in the Atlantic in a desperate effort to secure Europe." According to Admiral Bagley, former Commander-in-Chief of Naval Forces in Europe, Soviet naval capabilities relative to the United States will rise in the next 10-15 years as a result of newer programs, including the building of more corvettes armed with the SS-9 surface-to-surface missile with a range of 150 miles, 90 miles more than the American Harpoon missile; the introduction of a new class of destroyer escorts; expanded aircraft carrier construction; the potential deployment of V/STOL aircraft on *Moskva*-class helicopter cruisers; the production of laser weapons systems early in the 1980s; and an increase to 90 or 100 in the long-range Backfire bomber assigned to the Soviet Navy. The Soviet Union, which has more attack submarines than the United States, envisages their use primarily as missile carriers to attack surface ships in concert with land-based aircraft, such as the Backfire, and missile-armed surface vessels. In contrast, the United States regards attack submarines as having missions principally against enemy submarines. See Worth H. Bagley, *Sea Power and Western Security: The Next Decade* (London: International Institute for Strategic Studies, Adelphi Paper No. 139, Winter 1977).

[28]If, for example, West European governments, within existing budgetary constraints, were to devote greater resources to regions beyond Europe, they would take away from capabilities in Europe at a time when the Soviet Union is increasing its military strength in Europe relative to NATO.

24

United States and in Western Europe, of the military options that might be available, and necessary, to assure the supply of oil. The logic of the Alliance, if it were extended to extra-Atlantic security issues, would appear to lead to a systematic examination of the potential for, and the difficulties inherent in, the seizure of oil in order to forestall "economic strangulation," as well as the problems of protecting sea lanes through which commerce vital to the well-being of Western Europe and Japan must pass.[29] Such issues, discussed in a subsequent section of this Report, are set forth here not for the purpose of advocating a specific course of action—although the contingencies under which the use of force would become necessary have grown substantially as a result of events in Iran and Afghanistan, and it is difficult to envisage the noncommunist industrial world submitting supinely to actions by producer states, with or without Soviet complicity, whose effect would be to deprive industrialized states of their vital oil imports.

The problems confronting the United States and its industrialized allies in energy supply in the 1980s will have dimensions, especially in the short term, differing in several important aspects from the 1973-1974 period. The immediate problem may be that of assuring the flow of oil from producer countries in a region characterized by growing political instability. The longer-term issue, of course, remains the need to diversify energy supply by means of new technologies and policies both to exploit existing forms of energy, especially fossil fuels, and to find alternative energy sources. In the short term, the threat of massive energy disruptions resulting from political instability in the Persian Gulf may call for solutions that are essentially military in nature if the alternative is "economic strangulation," especially if such disruptions come at a time when the stockpiles of oil in the United States, Western Europe and Japan have already been depleted well below a sixty-day supply. Consideration of this option, stemming from the heightened potential for political instability in the Persian Gulf region, has become a more pressing need for industrialized oil-consuming states since the 1973-1974 period.

With such propositions and problems in mind, it is appropriate to examine each of the trends—political instability, energy supply-demand relationships, and the growth of Soviet power—likely to affect the energy supplies of the United States and its allies in the 1980s.

---

[29]Oil tankers account for one-fourth of the ships and 70 percent of the tonnage passing the Cape of Good Hope. About 18 million barrels of oil per day are carried in tankers from Persian Gulf ports around the Cape of Good Hope, most of it destined for markets in Western Europe or North America. By the 1980s as much as 60 percent of all U.S. oil imports may be shipped around the Cape of Good Hope.

3. Political Instability in the Persian Gulf

The potential for further political instability in the Persian Gulf beyond the Iranian revolution is enormous. The Islamic movement itself represents a force that is anti-Western and anti-secular, with a strong emphasis upon traditional values that contrast and conflict sharply with those of the proponents of political development and economic modernization. The Iranian revolution has not yet run its course, and the potential for violent reactions against modernizing forces exists elsewhere in oil-producing states of the Persian Gulf. Numerous groups contend for influence, power and control. The military has been gravely, and perhaps in the short run irreparably, weakened as a stabilizing and unifying force in Iran. In addition to well-armed radical leftists, the threat of ethnic separatism looms in Iran. The Kurds have seized control of regions near the Iranian-Iraqi border and have demanded autonomy within a federal Iranian state. This, in turn, is likely to encourage other separatist elements—for example, the Turks in Azerbaijan and the Baluchis in Eastern Iran—with attendant opportunities for external political manipulation. Even more uncertain is the future of the oil fields as a result of the Iranian revolution. The ultimate test for Iran may be the capacity of the government, whatever its political orientation, to exercise authority in the oil fields. The inability of the Shah's government to keep oil flowing contributed perhaps decisively to his downfall. Because of uncertainty about control of the oil fields, the future of Iranian oil production will be in doubt as long as the forces unleashed by the Iranian revolution remain active and uncontrolled. The departure of foreign technicians has already created serious technical problems of productive capacity and an "Iranians alone" policy could prevent recovery of 1977 levels until 1985.

The lifeline that sustains the supply of oil from the Persian Gulf to the United States and Western Europe is perilously fragile. Through the Strait of Hormuz, which is less than 30 miles wide, passes most of the oil produced by Saudi Arabia and other states in the Persian Gulf. Iran controls one side of the Strait of Hormuz which could be blocked by attacks against shipping (surface-to-surface missiles) launched from land or from warships or aircraft operating in the Persian Gulf. It should be noted that, contrary to some accounts, traffic through the Strait of Hormuz cannot be stopped simply by sinking a supertanker. The current channel in use is about five miles wide. Within the boundaries of this stretch of water, minimum depths average about 40 fathoms. This means that at least 240 feet separate the surface from the bottom. Even the largest tankers do not draw more than 90 feet when loaded, thus clearing the bottom and any obstructions by more than 125 feet. It is clear that one could sink tankers in the channel for days and not interrupt the traffic—outbound and, therefore, laden, as well as inbound. Moreover, 30-fathom water extends for miles beyond the normally employed channels.

Through the Strait of Hormuz passes not only Iranian oil, but also the far more important energy output of Saudi Arabia and other petroleum producers of the region—Kuwait, Qatar and the United Arab Emirates, the latter a loose federation of seven mini-states (Abu Dhabi, Dubai, Sharjah, Umm al-Qawain, Ras al-Khaimah, Ajman and Fujairah). Highly accurate weapons with devastating potential against a large target, such as a tanker, could be launched by relatively unskilled personnel, including small groups of insurgent forces operating in a politically volatile country, with or without the active encouragement of the central government or an external authority such as the Soviet Union. Hence, the geostrategic importance of Iran far transcends the oil that it can supply to, or withhold from, the world market.

The Musandam Peninsula, the tip of which is Omani territory, forms the other side of the Strait of Hormuz. This explains the intense Soviet interest in promoting the Dhofar rebellion in Western Oman, supplied from sanctuaries in South Yemen, and the equal British and Iranian interest in helping Sultan Qaboos suppress the insurrection. Moreover, there remains the question of the future of Abu Musa and the Tunbs Islands, seized by Iran following the British withdrawal from the Gulf in 1971. Will they be retained by Iran? If so, much will depend upon the nature of the government which eventually emerges from the Iranian revolution. Their importance lies in the fact that they dominate egress from the Gulf.

It is evident that the security problems facing the United States and its allies have increased to an extent not fully understood. The political transformation in Iran has removed a local stabilizing force whose interest lay in assuring the unimpeded access of shipping to the Persian Gulf as well as stability within the states of the region. The inability or the unwillingness of Iran to play a role as "regional policeman" compounds the uncertainties that beset the Persian Gulf as a result of recent events. This fundamental shift in Iranian policy—from stabilizing influence to a proponent of radical change—is likely to give rise to unrest in neighboring states, the revival of old border disputes, and the emergence or resuscitation of rivalries among states in the region.

In the years since the 1975 OPEC meeting in Algiers, with its peripheral Iraqi-Iranian agreement, Iraq had enjoyed an improved working relationship with the Shah, which led to a reduction of Iraqi-Iranian hostilities in general and to the termination of the Kurdish revolt against Baghdad.

Now, with renewed insurgency among Iranian Kurds in the wake of the Shah's departure, Iraq no less than Iran may soon face another revolt in its own Kurdish district, especially since Iraqi moves to "Arabize" this area by means of forced immigration have done little to improve relations with the Kurdish community. Iraq also has reason to fear the Islamic revival that plays so important a role in Iran's revolution, since the majority (54 percent) of Iraq's population is Shiite Moslem, while the Iraqi leadership remains predominantly Sunni. Encouraged by the Iranian example (and remembering Iraq's earlier expulsion of Khomeini at the behest of the Shah), Shiite dissidents may become more active. Given the recent (and often bloody) Iraqi-PLO feud, the support for the PLO in Iran under the Ayatollah Khomeini cannot be entirely pleasing to Baghdad. The costs of the Iranian revolution to Iraq (e.g., rising prospect of Iraqi domestic unrest) probably will outweigh the potential benefits (e.g., a freer Iraqi hand in the Gulf, at least over the short term).

Internally, Saudi Arabia faces, or soon will confront, many of the socio-economic pressures that accompany modernization and led to the Shah's downfall. Rising economic and political expectations, increased Westernization and urbanization, corruption and inefficiency, infrastructure bottlenecks and the need for immigrant labor are present in Saudi Arabia, although perhaps on a lesser scale than in Iran under the Shah. But together they are likely to pose severe problems for the Saudi monarchy. Because of its support for Islamic fundamentalism, the Saudi royal family may be less susceptible than the Shah to religious opposition. Because of the *majlis* tradition of public audiences, the Saudi rulers are undoubtedly in closer touch with their subjects than was the Shah. However, against the background of the Iranian upheaval, the Saudi leadership may feel compelled to move more quickly, and with less certain consequences, toward greater democratization.

Aside from the overall tensions of modernization, the most likely source of domestic unrest in Saudi Arabia, as in Kuwait, is the large expatriate labor force, drawn mostly from the poorer Arab and Islamic states (especially the Yemens) and now numbering some 1,500,000—and which, from the Soviet perspective, is said to constitute a large, strategically placed "proletariat" ripe for exploitation in the charged political environment of the region. The Saudis have tried to prevent any one national group from becoming too prominent, and have generally isolated immigrant enclaves from Saudi political centers. But such workers, increasingly dissatisfied with their living conditions and wage levels, have precipitated occasional strikes and riots. They may be particularly vulnerable to political radicalization prompted by Egyptian exiles and Palestinian elements or to subversion from radical neighbors such as Iraq, South Yemen and Ethiopia. They may provide considerable disruptive potential for exploitation by the Soviet Union.

Even in the absence of domestic unrest, the Saudi leadership is likely to face increasing pressure from external sources of instability and conflict. Aside from the prospect of becoming entangled in the Arab "eastern front" with Israel, recent Saudi fears have centered on potential Iraqi threats (perhaps spurred by Soviet manipulation) to Kuwait's territorial integrity and her oil industry infrastructure. With the security guarantee extended by the Shah to Kuwait removed, Saudi Arabia will find it more difficult than in the past to avoid involvement in any Iraq-Kuwait conflict. Saudi concern for the stability of Kuwait coincides with Saudi interest in maintaining access to, and influence in, the lesser Gulf states, such as Bahrain, Qatar and the United Arab Emirates, which provide Riyadh with overland routes to Persian Gulf ports and important financial and tele-communications centers. In the 1980s, incipient rivalries within and among these states, focused primarily on commercial competition and unsettled border disputes, and fueled by tribal tensions and radicaliza-tion among the large foreign worker force, could make imperative a Saudi political-military response. The situation could become even worse in Oman and the two Yemens along the southern coast of the Arabian Peninsula, where the effects of Iranian retrenchment may help to revive and deepen the domestic and interstate conflict, thereby jeopardizing Saudi plans for port access on the Indian Ocean (via Oman or North Yemen) and drawing Riyadh into local hostilities. In fact, the recent clashes between North and South Yemen have done just that.

Thus, Saudi Arabia probably will be called upon to play a larger regional security role, particularly with respect to the air and sea lines of com-munication along the Persian Gulf and the Red Sea. Whether the Saudis can do so without substantial Western military assistance, and still with-stand domestic destabilizing forces that are likely to grow as a result of a rapid military buildup, remains uncertain. As the impetus for such a regional role for Saudi Arabia rises, so will the problems created by the country's growing vulnerability to revolutionary forces.

Trends in North Yemen and in South Yemen pose security threats to Saudi Arabia. The Soviet Union, the German Democratic Republic and Cuba are said to have as many as 1,500 advisers and other personnel in South Yemen. In early 1979, Soviet, Cuban and East German advisers moved quickly to provide assistance to Marxist South Yemen, and Saudi forces, encouraged by the United States, took steps to shore up the pro-Western North Yemeni regime. The United States accelerated military assistance to North Yemen. By August 1979, however, the Soviet Union had shipped arms to North Yemen after a visit to Moscow by a delegation that included North Yemen's defense minister and chief of staff. The Soviet Union has furnished substantial amounts of anti-aircraft and anti-tank missiles, sub-machine guns, mortars and ammunition. Moscow is said to have prom-ised to provide MiG-21 aircraft and T-62 tanks to North Yemen.

Both Yemens suffer from internal strains which could either prompt do-mestic strife or propel them toward prolonged conflict. Instability in North Yemen, largely the by-product of traditional tribal religious tensions, has been virtually constant since the civil war of the early 1960s. The current border war between North and South Yemen has its origins in both internal and external factors. Moreover, given the radical Marxist orientation of the South Yemen regime, it was perhaps inevitable that Saudi Arabia would seek to prop up the shaky government in North Yemen. The Saudis have a direct interest in keeping the increasingly important Red Sea port of Al Mukha (developed by Iran) out of radical hands.

In view of the unfolding scenario in the Yemens, Saudi plans for access to the Indian Ocean (bypassing the Strait of Hormuz) via the Red Sea through Bab el Mandeb probably must be shelved, although uncertain-ties surrounding the Strait of Hormuz increase the need for an alternative route for Saudi Arabian oil exports. As a result, Oman's importance for Saudi sea access has increased dramatically. However, as in the case of North Yemen, Oman has long faced domestic unrest. The stability of this strategically-placed, conservative sultanate lies in doubt. With the fall of the Shah and the withdrawal of the remaining Iranian troops from Oman, the Dhofar rebellion, led by the South Yemeni-backed Popular Front for the Liberation of Oman (PFLO), may be revived with potential geostrategic consequences for control of the Strait of Hormuz noted above. The PFLO also could provide a means for the northward extension of South Yemen (and, by implication, Cuban-Soviet) influence to the Persian Gulf flank of the Arabian Peninsula.

Apart from the possible loss of modest port/naval facilities in Muscat and Rakhyut, renewed civil war holds ominous implications for Oman's longer-term economic and political interests since new discoveries—both light and heavy crude—have turned up in Dhofar, inland from Sal-alah. Apparently it has long been known that there was oil in this region but it had been thought to be expensive to extract and ship out. Present plans are to build a pipeline from this new field to the existing one north of Muscat and pump the crude through the existing loading terminal.

There are also ample sources of conflict within and among the lesser Gulf states, even though they have enjoyed a period of stability in recent years. The United Arab Emirates is subject to centrifugal forces which could pull the federation apart. The two most influential states—Abu Dhabi and Dubai—continue to compete for economic and political preeminence. Dubai, which enjoys the best harbor facilities, was the favored state during the days of British rule and now aspires to a larger role in the federation. However, thanks to its phenomenal population growth (600 percent between 1965 and 1976) and oil wealth, Abu Dhabi has emerged as the dominant state in the United Arab Emirates, and its ruler—Shaikh Zayed—serves as President. Unfortunately, the on-going rivalry between Dubai and Abu Dhabi has hampered UAE attempts at economic cooperation and has heightened tensions over moves to form a unified army and police structure. It also holds the seeds for external political and military intervention, as Dubai has sought an ally in Iran to counter the increasingly close relationship between Abu Dhabi and Saudi Arabia. In this regard, the coastal traders of Dubai have always been more cosmopolitan and secular, and less traditional, and could conceivably provide a beachhead for radical political activities from across the Gulf.

But as in other Gulf states, foreign labor, which accounts for some 80 percent of the UAE's total population, presents probably the greatest threat to political stability. Radicalization, sparked mainly by Palestinian elements, has increased steadily and could easily lead to domestic unrest, especially since the PLO now enjoys a sanctuary base in nearby Iran and may have at its disposal unprecedented levels of armaments and financial support from the Iranian revolutionary government. The absence of clearly demarcated frontiers could lead to hostilities between the United Arab Emirates and adjacent states, particularly in cases such as the Ras al-Khaimah/Oman dispute over control of vital resources and sea lanes. In the wake of internal turmoil in Iran, Ras al-Khaimah may once again press its claim over the Tunb Islands and Abu Musa in the Strait of Hormuz, which were seized by the Shah in 1971. Although presumably settled via the good offices of Saudi Arabia, disputes over the land and maritime boundaries separating Qatar and Abu Dhabi may also reemerge. This, in turn, could rekindle the tripartite debate among Saudi Arabia, the UAE and Oman over final control in the Buraimi Oasis, a rare source of fresh water located on the UAE-Oman border.

To the north of the UAE, Qatar and Bahrain also suffer from the foreign worker problem, though Bahrain is less vulnerable than Qatar (where immigrants make up 60 percent of manpower). Territorial disputes between these two states could become more intense, as Bahrain still claims the island of Hawar off the west coast of the Qatar Peninsula.

Bahrain alone, however, will remain the most likely flash point for external conflict. Composed of some thirty islands, Bahrain is one of the key commercial-communications centers in the Persian Gulf, providing a range of advanced banking, trade and harbor facilities, a huge new drydock and ship repair installation, and perhaps the best communications services in the Gulf region. It also maintains large fresh water resources. Among the surrounding Arab states (especially Saudi Arabia), access to (and influence on) Bahrain is considered essential. For this reason alone, this island state constitutes a lucrative target for forces bent on inciting instability in the Gulf region. The fact that the Bahraini Moslem population is roughly 50 percent Shiite, in a world dominated by Sunni Islam, might provide a lever for external manipulation, perhaps by a radical Iran. Yet there have been traditionally close relations between Bahrain and the U.S. Middle East force—a small naval force present in the Persian Gulf, the Red Sea and western Indian Ocean—and there is an on-going development of special links (including a new causeway) between Bahrain and Saudi Arabia.

The Use of Force: Contingencies and Constraints

It has been noted above that, for the United States and its allies in the 1973-1974 period, solutions of a unilateral nature—usually arms for oil—took precedence in the short term as stop-gap measures over the creation of multilateral frameworks for collaborative action. Military force, too, is an option likely to be exercised only in contingencies in which other solutions are foreclosed by virtue of inadequate time, a problem that is more likely than ever before to confront the United States and its allies in the 1980s. If, for example, the Persian Gulf were to be blocked through the domination of the Strait of Hormuz, or Saudi oil production were to be denied the West for some other reason, time would not be available to find and develop alternative sources of energy. This would assume that stockpiles of oil held by industrialized states, presently constituting about 60-90 days supply, had been drawn down. Thus, use of force would provide perhaps the only immediate option. But would such action be taken by the United States and several of its allies, or by the United States alone, or by its allies alone?

It is difficult, and perhaps impossible, to envisage the Atlantic Alliance, in the form of a unanimous agreement in the North Atlantic Council, taking a decision to use force to seize Persian Gulf oil. Less implausible would be concerted military action, taken by the United States and certain of its allies, in the changed circumstances that may confront oil-consuming states in the 1980s. But which ones? Britain will be a net oil exporter in the 1980s and, therefore, not subject to "economic strangulation" in this period by the curtailment of oil supply unless North Sea oil is disrupted, as could happen as a result of sabotage or in a wartime situation. The Federal Republic of Germany and France represent the other principal West European states whose military potential, in theory at least, could be used in conjunction with U.S. forces. But the FRG has developed military forces entirely for use on the NATO Central Front, differing both in geography and military problems from the Persian Gulf, and the Federal Republic is prohibited by its Basic Law, or constitution, from using its military power outside the North Atlantic area. Since 1966, France has been formally outside the NATO command structure, although there has been continuing and growing defense collaboration between French, U.S. and other NATO forces, and France maintains a naval force, periodically including an aircraft carrier, in the Indian Ocean. Britain may be prepared, under the Thatcher Government, to station occasionally a squadron consisting of a helicopter cruiser, frigates, and a nuclear attack submarine "East of Suez." Early in 1980, Britain deployed four destroyers in the Mediterranean as the United States drew units from the Sixth Fleet to the Indian Ocean.

In light of the major sources of political instability in the Persian Gulf, and their potential implications for energy supply in the 1980s, several contingencies can be postulated in which the use of military power could become necessary. These include attacks against tankers by warships and aircraft operating in the Persian Gulf; destruction of such shipping by the laying of mines, thus closing the Strait of Hormuz; and attacks against shipping by means of weapons used by forces operating ashore. A revolutionary change in Saudi Arabia—as a result of which production ceased or slowed greatly in what constitutes the largest source of oil from the Persian Gulf—represents another contingency in which the use of force would become a prominent option. These contingencies are by no means mutually exclusive; combinations of them could occur simultaneously. The problems inherent in the use of military force increase in complexity, difficulty and uncertainty, from the first to the last contingency.

In the first contingency—the harassment of tanker traffic from naval or air craft—a naval task force, perhaps comprising both U.S. units and some from other Atlantic Alliance members, could be formed to provide convoy protection and to remove mines. Such a force would be interposed between tankers and potentially hostile craft, upon which the burden of escalating to the overt use of force would be placed. Thus, the deployment of military power as a deterrent to attack against tankers could be envisaged.

In the second contingency, the need would exist to destroy shore installations and groups of forces posing a threat to the narrow sea lines of communications through the Strait of Hormuz. Air strikes against such forces could be mounted from carrier-based aircraft or from bases on land, if available. But this contingency raises at least the possibility of military action to seize and occupy one or both of the strategically important littorals of the Strait of Hormuz. Whether such action could be mounted with Alliance support is problematical. But it is a contingency deserving of consideration in an Alliance context.

The most formidable of the problems for the United States and its allies, from both a political and military perspective, would arise in the event of revolutionary change or prolonged political instability in Saudi Arabia resulting in the curtailment of oil production. To be effective, military power would have to be used to preempt the destruction of oil-producing facilities, including sabotage of the oil wells themselves and damage to pipelines and other technological infrastructure. The decision to use such force would have to be weighed carefully against the sabotage potential that would exist during and after the seizure of the oil fields and local production facilities. Because of its inherent problems, as well as the stakes involved and the difficult and perhaps desperate political-military conditions under which it would be undertaken, this contingency should be the object of consideration and planning by those Alliance members having a stake in oil supply from the region.

In the 1980s, Western Europe and Japan will remain more heavily dependent than the United States upon imports for their aggregate energy supply. At the same time, the energy-import dependence of the United States will exceed 50 percent of its total energy consumption, in the absence of a rapid increase in U.S. domestic production or the curtailment of demand through stringent conservation measures. Paradoxically, the effect of trends in U.S. oil imports since the 1973-1974 period has been to narrow the gap that, at the beginning of the 1970s, separated the United States and its allies—Western Europe and Japan—in levels of oil-import dependence. If the growth of U.S. dependence has heightened the potential for competition among industrialized states for Persian Gulf oil that may be in short supply, it has also increased the commonality of interest among the United States, Western Europe and Japan in assuring the continued flow of that oil. But the question remains whether Western Europe, especially the energy-import dependent states of the Continent, would be prepared to support, tacitly, perhaps with at least token contributions of military capabilities, the use of force to secure access to oil vital to the economic survival of the noncommunist industrialized world. This would assume that nonmilitary options had been exhausted, or were irrelevant in light of the immediate problems of assuring energy supply facing the United States and its allies.

In sum, the problems of energy have grown greatly in complexity since the 1973-1974 period. Compared with that period, the United States today confronts a situation in which anti-Western, and specifically anti-American, forces have multiplied almost in direct proportion to the growth of U.S. dependence on oil imports from the Persian Gulf. These trends have coincided with vast increases in Soviet military power—strategic-nuclear and general purpose forces—relative to the United States and Western Europe, thus complicating immensely for the West the problems of protecting their vital interests in the Persian Gulf, and even enhancing considerably the potential for Soviet miscalculation about their resolve in a crisis in any one of the contingencies outlined above.

4. Oil Supply-Demand Relationships

Against projections of political instability in the Persian Gulf region must be set oil supply-demand relationships in the 1980s. The idea of resource scarcity long antedates the present era. Rapidly accelerating rates of energy utilization associated with the Industrial Revolution led in the nineteenth century to Malthusian projections that population growth and consequent pressures upon finite resources would eventually depress living standards. Technology would allegedly place increased demands upon existing resources, while population growth, including longer life spans, would lead to scarcities of food and other commodities and resources vital to man's well-being.

For example, W. Stanley Jevons wrote in 1865 that the continued growth of coal consumption in Britain at a 3.5 percent annual rate could not be sustained. He suggested that

We cannot long maintain our present rate of increase of consumption; . . . we can never advance to the higher amounts of consumption supposed. But this only means that the check to our progress must become perceptible within a century from the present time; that the cost of fuel must rise, perhaps within a lifetime, to a rate injurious to our commercial and manufacturing supremacy; and the conclusion is inevitable, that our present happy progressive condition is a thing of limited duration.[30]

In point of fact, coal consumption increased more slowly in Britain in the second half of the nineteenth century than in the first half as the pace of innovation in the Industrial Revolution in Britain slackened and as the efficiency of steam engines improved. But coal did not become a source of energy because supplies of wood were about to be exhausted, just as oil was not sought as a substitute for coal. Alternative energy sources have not been consciously planned to be available as substitutes for an existing form of energy that is about to be exhausted. The reasons for the expansion of oil as a source of energy, as opposed to coal, stemmed from factors which included more efficient methods of handling (storage, transport and utilization) along with its incredibly low price. If to these factors are added the then seemingly inexhaustible supply, it was inevitable that oil would supplant coal as a primary energy source. In the longer term, of course, the shift to other forms of energy such as oil has weakened demand for an existing source such as coal. Nevertheless, the idea of the exhaustion of resources is not new, although it appeared in

---

[30]W. Stanley Jevons, *The Coal Question* (London: MacMillan, 1861); quoted in John Maddox, *Beyond the Energy Crisis: A Global Perspective* (New York: McGraw Hill, 1975), pp. 25-26.

the 1970s in the form of hypotheses and forecasts of ecological disaster and the consequent advocacy of "zero rates of growth," and as a set of problems for industrialized states created by their dependence on energy sources located in politically volatile regions beyond their control.

Traditional and contemporary projections of resource exhaustion and population increase are usually linked to conceptions of finite resources that will be exhausted later, if not sooner. Both in the case of coal and other resources, however, predictions of imminent disaster because of depletion have proven premature. Demand has slowed as substitutes have been found. Technology has altered the relative importance of one resource as compared with another. For this reason, raw material-producing countries have often faced widely fluctuating demand for their exports, and economic planners have sought, through industrialization and export diversification, to lessen dependence on one commodity.

If historical precedents are instructive, the problem of energy supply is related directly to the ability to find satisfactory substitutes and to make them economically and technologically feasible at the appropriate point in time. Thus, political and economic projections are fraught with considerable potential for error. In order to assess the implications of resource issues for industrialized states, it is necessary to develop assumptions based on alternative projections of resource dependence and energy demand and supply. For example, such projections must contain a series of assumptions about economic growth and demand for oil and other forms of energy in consuming countries, as well as availability of oil supplies and, especially in the next decade, the ability and the willingness of major producers, notably Saudi Arabia, to increase production— a variable fraught with similar uncertainty. At the same time, it is necessary to engage in technological forecasting to ascertain the extent to which alternative energy sources will become available, or could be developed, together with the necessary lead-times.

On the one hand, our economic assumptions about future demand/supply relationships for oil are dependent on levels of production and the extractive capacity of producers within a specified time period, say between 1980 and 1985. Projections of supply are based upon data about oil reserves that can be extracted within the timeframe of the projection. As one analysis has suggested: "For prudent planning, therefore, the best available guide to supply levels over the coming decade will remain the volume of reserves already proved—without making any allowance for reserves that might be brought to light through an intensified or redirected drilling effort."[31] Various higher or lower sets of figures are available, but "even the lower figures are fraught with so much uncertainty that they form a perilous platform for long-term supply or price forecasts."[32] On the other hand, the adequacy of energy supply relative to demand is related also to the ability of consumers to develop effective conservation policies. It is dependent upon elasticity of demand. The imposition of the "world price" of oil upon the U.S. market has been advocated as a constraint on American demand. One recent study has concluded that the United States could reduce its energy consumption by as much as 30 or 40 percent with little or no adverse effect on living standards. Such would be the result of steadily rising real prices, incentives toward conservation, and information and educational campaigns designed to reduce the use of oil.[33]

But energy projections are dependent upon *political* factors as much as they are related to economic issues. Most important may not be whether or not fossil fuels exist in known fields in the Middle East or elsewhere, but instead the political environment within and among oil-producing states, as the Iranian crisis vividly demonstrates, or at a broader international level, as illustrated dramatically in 1973-1974. In light of the preceding survey of political trends within and among major oil-producing states in the Persian Gulf, the likelihood of political factors influencing decisively the availability of oil in the 1980s looms large. Thus, alternative political scenarios ultimately determine supply/demand projections based on economic factors. Both are essential to an adequate understanding of the implications of energy for industrialized states in the 1980s.

If the emerging political environment of the 1980s does not augur well for the reliability of projections confined to economic factors, such projections are useful, nevertheless, in setting parameters of the energy problems facing industrialized states that would exist even in the absence of political uncertainty. Japan and Western Europe as a whole (excepting, of course, Norway and the United Kingdom) may remain dependent upon oil imports in the 1980s at levels comparable to the late 1970s, although such a projection must be based upon variables such as economic growth and the success of energy conservation. With the exceptions noted, indigenous sources of energy and programs of conservation will

---

[31]"Oil Supplies—Deluge or Drought?," *Petroleum Economist*, October 1978, p. 407.
[32]*Loc. cit.*
[33]See Daniel Yergin, "Conservation, The Key Energy Source," in Robert Stobaugh and Daniel Yergin, editors, *Energy Future: Report of the Energy Project at the Harvard Business School* (New York: Random House, 1979), p. 182.

probably be adequate at best to reduce only marginally existing levels of dependence on imports within the next decade. Although Western Europe and Japan may make increased funding available for research for alternative sources of energy, technological breakthroughs, even if they were to come about, would not affect greatly the availability of energy in the 1980s. For at least the next decade, no other sources of energy will have as great versatility as oil to satisfy the diverse needs of the United States and other consuming nations. As one analyst has observed: "Oil can be substituted for gas as a boiler fuel with minor conversion costs and pipeline grade gas can be produced from the light ends of liquid petroleum. Oil will do most anything that coal will do with less cost. The converse is not true. Very substantial costs are involved in the conversion of coal to serve the petroleum or gas energy purpose."[34] But it has also been suggested that solar energy could provide as much as one-quarter of the energy needs of the United States by the end of the century.[35] However, it should be noted that South Africa has plans to become oil-independent by the mid-1980s simply by converting its vast coal reserves to petroleum and all the other derivatives which come as dividends in the process.

The International Energy Agency has projected total import needs of IEA members in 1985 at between 42 and 48 million barrels of oil per day, substantially in excess of total OPEC production of 36 to 38 million barrels daily. This is based on an average annual growth rate of 4.3 percent. It is assumed that equilibrium between supply and demand—a shortfall of between 4 and 12 million barrels—will be achieved by oil price increases.[36]

In another study, it is assumed that the growth rate of energy needs in noncommunist states will fall from an average of 4.2 percent per year in 1975-1980 to 3.3 percent in 1980-1985 and to 3 percent per year in 1985-1990. But oil supplies may not increase sufficiently to keep pace with even these reduced rates of increase in oil-consuming states, or to provide a margin of reserves in the event of further cutbacks in production resulting from political instability in oil-producing states. World oil supplies are projected to rise from their 44.6 million barrels per day level of

[34]Samuel M. Dix, *Energy: A Critical Decision for the United States Economy* (Grand Rapids, Michigan: Energy Education Publishers, 1977), p. 41.
[35]For an extended discussion of the issue of solar energy, see Modesto A. Maidique, "Solar America," in Stobaugh and Yergin, editors, *op. cit.*, pp. 183-215; Daniel Yergin, "U.S. Energy Policy: Transits to What?," *The World Today*, March 1979, pp. 81-91.
[36]See Walter J. Levy, "The Years that the Locust Hath Eaten: Oil Policy and OPEC Development Prospects," *Foreign Affairs*, Winter 1978-1979, p. 289.

1975 to 62.5 million in 1985, and 65.4 million in 1990.[37] Of this total, OPEC members will account for no more than 36.5 million barrels per day, both in 1985 and 1990—a figure that accords substantially with the OPEC production estimate set forth in the IEA report noted above. (This figure also corresponds to the projection contained in the analysis undertaken by the Workshop on Alternative Energy Strategies.)[38] Oil consumption in the noncommunist world was anticipated to increase to 61.5 million barrels in 1985, and 64.4 in 1990. Although the 1985 figure of 61.5 million barrels per day is substantially below the 68-72 million barrels per day contained in the controversial CIA study of 1977, the margin between production and demand is slim indeed.

Without Iranian production, world oil supplies would fall short of projected 1979 consumption by at least one million barrels a day.[39] Even with full Iranian production of 6.5 million barrels a day, the margin between production and demand would leave no room either for modest increases in economic growth rates or for political scenarios in which one or more other major oil producers cut back production, as occurred in Iran in 1978-1979—and similar cutbacks must probably be anticipated in the 1980s as the potential for political instability in the Persian Gulf increases. It has been suggested that Saudi Arabia may not possess a sustainable production capacity in excess of 9.5 million barrels a day because of such technical problems as lower pressure and rising gas-oil ratios in the Ghawar field.[40] As Table 2 indicates, other OPEC members do not have excess capacity with which to compensate for a decline in production by one or more states such as Iran. Moreover, reductions could materialize as a result of decisions taken by oil-producing states to restrict production, either because they lack absorptive capacity for oil revenues in domestic projects, or because they reject the secularization that usually accompanies modernization as manifest in the traditionalism of the Islamic revolution. In short, the CIA study of 1977 noted above provides a "best case" political analysis, even though the prospects for the 1980s warrant a pessimistic prognosis.

---

[37]*A Technical Analysis of the International Oil Market* (London: Petroleum Economics Limited, 1978). See also E. Stanley Tucker, "World Energy Supplies: New Study Previews the 1980s," *Petroleum Economist*, October 1978, p. 426.

[38]*Energy: Global Prospects 1985-2000*, Report of the Workshop on Alternative Energy Strategies (New York: McGraw Hill, 1977), esp. pp. 3-46.

[39]"The Damage from Iran," *Fortune*, March 12, 1979, p. 12.

[40]Daniel I. Fine, "Saudi Oil Production: A Serious Short-Term Problem?," *Business Week*, December 10, 1979, pp. 52-53.

TABLE 2
OPEC's Spare Capacity is Razor-Thin
(thousands of barrels per day)

	Maximum Sustainable Capacity	Production	Excess Capacity
		August 1979	
Saudi Arabia	9,800[1]	9,500	29
Kuwait	2,800	2,524	276
United Arab Emirates	2,360	1,731	529
Qatar	600	533	67
Iraq	3,000	3,500	(500)[2]
Libya	2,200	1,989	211
Venezuela	2,400	2,330	70
Nigeria	2,400	2,300	100
Indonesia	1,650	1,600	50
Algeria	1,100	1,225	(125)[2]
Other OPEC countries	450	445	5
Total OPEC minus Iran	28,760	27,677	1,337
Iran	5,500	3,500	2,000
Total OPEC	34,260	31,177	3,337

[1]Includes neutral zone on Saudi-Kuwait border
[2]Temporary production beyond sustainable capacity

Source: World Energy Project, Massachusetts Institute of Technology

Supply Trends

It has been estimated that, in order to keep pace with world demand for oil in the next decade, it would be necessary to have discovered another North Sea- or Alaskan-size oil deposit every three years over the past decade, since it takes at least a decade to bring new oil discoveries into production. As the Commission of the European Community, in a judiciously worded statement, put it:

Whereas during the period 1960-70 there was a relative surplus of energy, the market in the future will be subject to more difficult conditions which would lead to major problems of supply at certain times and in certain areas. . . . The energy market—both in the Community and world-wide—will, therefore, become more insecure than it has been in the past. The most difficult period may well be the next 10-15 years. In particular, additional petroleum imports required by the three great consumers—the USA, Japan, and Western Europe—will in 1980 run to 1,300 million tons compared with 1970; this figure is so high that the question inevitably arises as to whether and how the available geological reserves can be discovered and exploited in time.[41]

Moreover, the petroleum available to consuming states in the mid-1980s will come from reserves which have already been identified. Walter Levy has suggested that, even with an average annual rate of discovery of 18 to 20 billion barrels of oil in 1985, "the production-to-reserves ratio would decline from 32 years in 1978 to 25 years in 1985."[42] It is estimated that, within the next decade, the United States will not be able to increase substantially its domestic production of oil. Accordingly, "In the late 1980s, only 5 million barrels a day are likely to come from reserves that were known to exist in 1978, including Alaska. It is unlikely that U.S. production in the late 1980s will include more than 4 million barrels daily of oil from new fields found between 1978 and the late 1980s. And even this is a high estimate."[43]

One recent analysis suggests that the question is not whether substantial amounts of oil remain to be discovered, but rather how much oil can be extracted by more efficient methods. Current recovery rates are approximately 25-35 percent and "enhanced" recovery may add no more than 10 percent. Of even more fundamental importance is the extent to which exploratory drilling can yield what have been termed super-giant or giant oil fields.[44] It has been suggested that the "importance of super-giant fields is paralleled by their rarity" and that of the 33 identified, 25 were in the Middle East.[45] Outside the Middle East, the most promising prospect seems to be in the Reforma area of Mexico, with oil both onshore and offshore—with a combination of tangential structures with very thick reservoirs."[46] Since the 1960s, the discovery rate of large new oil fields has dropped greatly. "Onshore discoveries have already begun to de-

---

[41]Commission of the European Communities, *Problems, Resources and Necessary Progress in Community Energy Policy 1975-1985* (Luxembourg: Office for Official Publications of the European Community), p. 25.

[42]Levy, *op. cit.*, p. 290.

[43]Robert Stobaugh, "After the Peak: The Threat of Imported Oil," in Stobaugh and Yergin, editors, *op. cit.*, p. 42.

[44]A super-giant oil field has been defined as containing at least 5 billion barrels of known recoverable crude oil; a giant oil field is one from which it is expected that at least 500 million barrels can be extracted. Richard Nehring, *Giant Oil Fields and World Oil Resources*, prepared for the Central Intelligence Agency (Santa Monica, Calif.: The Rand Corporation, R2284-CIA, 1978), pp. 6-7.

[45]*Ibid.*, p. 62.

[46]*Ibid.*, p. 63.

cline sharply. The number of known and probable giant fields other than super-giants discovered onshore peaked in the early 1960s at 31. By the early 1970s, it had dropped back to 18. Offshore giant discoveries probably peaked at 27 in the early 1970s and are likely to begin to decline either in the late 1970s or the early 1980s."[47] The discovery of vast new deposits would have little effect on production levels within the next decade because of the several years lead-time in extracting oil and bringing it to market.

Since the early 1960s, there have been no new discoveries of large oil reserves except in Libya, Algeria, the North Sea, Alaska and Mexico, and none of these equals the reserves available now, or likely to be available within the next decade, from the Middle East. North America and Western Europe contain only about 12 percent of world reserves. The major oil still to be tapped is said to lie in either the Soviet Union or the People's Republic of China.[48] But the rate of discovery is likely to continue to decline in the remaining years of this century, even though advances in drilling technology can be expected. In short, the prospect of discovering oil in the quantity found in the Middle East appears remote,[49] with only Mexico possibly offering the prospect of oil reserves approximating those of Saudi Arabia[50]—though they may turn out to be comparable only to those of Iran. The effect of Mexican oil in such quantities, if the prognosis is accurate, would lessen substantially the dependence of the United States and other consuming states on the Middle East and provide some

---

[47]*Ibid.*, p. 65.
[48]"World total recoverable reserves of 2 trillion barrels are believed to exist; 55 percent or 1.1 trillion barrels have already been discovered . . . Of the 1.1 trillion barrels of discovered ultimately recoverable reserves (proven plus probable) some 513 billion (47 percent) are located in the Middle East. . . . Of the 925 billion barrels thought still to be discovered, 33 percent may be located in the Communist countries—principally the USSR and China; 17 percent may be found in the Middle East and less than a quarter of this undiscovered reserve might be found in North America, Western Europe, and Japan combined." *Geopolitics of Energy*, printed at the request of Henry M. Jackson, Chairman, Committee on Interior and Insular Affairs, United States Senate, Energy Publication No. 95-1, January 1977 (Washington: U.S. Government Printing Office, 1977), p. 32.
[49]As the Report of the Workshop on Alternative Energy Strategies, *Energy: Global Prospects 1985-2000, op. cit.* (p. 123), noted: "New techniques of assessing prospective regions make it possible to identify structures that might contain large oil accumulations. These are the areas that will be drilled first, and, as the search moves into less likely areas, the discovery rate will probably decline. . . . Over 30,000 oil fields have been discovered, but about 75% of the oil lies within 240 large fields, each with over 500 million barrels of recoverable reserves. All the effort put into oil exploration around the world over the past one hundred years has only yielded 240 large oil fields."
[50]James Nelson Goodsell, "Mexico: The Next Oil Power," *Christian Science Monitor*, November 16, 1978, p. 1.

additional time to make necessary adaptations in energy utilization from the present emphasis on oil to other forms of energy. Mexico could produce seven million barrels a day but will probably control output to levels around three to four million at best to avoid Iranian "mistakes." Here again, however, political considerations may outweigh economic factors. The level of Mexico's oil and natural gas production is likely to be influenced by issues other than an international market dominated by U.S. demand.

The Carter Administration's analysis of the limits of Saudi Arabian production completed in 1977 was based more upon economic than political considerations. The growth in political instability in the Persian Gulf region holds ominous implications for Saudi Arabia. To be sure, as numerous analysts have suggested, the internal differences between Iran and Saudi Arabia are considerable. To a far greater extent than was Iran under the Shah, Saudi Arabia remains a traditional society. But Saudi Arabia, encompassing a huge geographic area of 873,972 square miles—one-quarter the size of the United States—has a population of less than 8 million, substantially below that of the New York metropolitan area. Its frontiers are not easily defensible. The concentration of its oil fields makes them subject to sabotage and perhaps even seizure by revolutionary forces. In any event, the growth of Soviet influence in states around Saudi Arabia, together with the precipitous decline in U.S. influence symbolized by the ouster of the Shah, creates for Saudi Arabia a new set of problems which will impinge on its oil policies.

The world's major remaining reserves of natural gas lie principally in the Soviet Union and the Middle East, and possibly in the Arctic, including regions outside the Soviet Union.[51] Despite the temporary reversal of declining domestic production resulting from the flow of natural gas from the new Alaskan fields, the United States will probably experience a fall in domestic production of natural gas for most of the remaining years of this century. Although Western Europe currently is able to meet its natural gas needs from domestic reserves, the future prospects are less than sanguine. Thus, the likelihood exists that, by the late 1980s, both Western Europe and the United States will face increasing energy problems related to natural gas; and, if this is the case, only a substantial increase in the use of other energy sources could erode significantly the relative importance of petroleum for world energy needs by the 1990s.[52]

---

[51]The Soviet Union may contain as much as 36 percent and the Middle East, principally Iran, may hold as much as 24 percent, with 14 percent in North America and about 10 percent in Western Europe. See *Geopolitics of Energy, op. cit.*, p. 70.
[52]*Ibid.*, p. 26.

If the various projections about energy supply-demand relationships are compared, what emerges is a substantial level of consensus about the conditions that will face the United States and other energy import-dependent states in the 1980s. A large number of such projections were prepared in the 1974-1976 period, and others were completed in 1977-1978. The earlier conclusion was that declining economic growth rates would result in lower rates of increase in energy consumption and greater energy demand elasticity, producing a gradual decline in energy imports. In later studies, there has been an upward revision in projections for net oil imports because of reductions in forecasted indigenous energy supply—which does not augur well for efforts to reduce drastically our imports of oil in the years just ahead.[53]

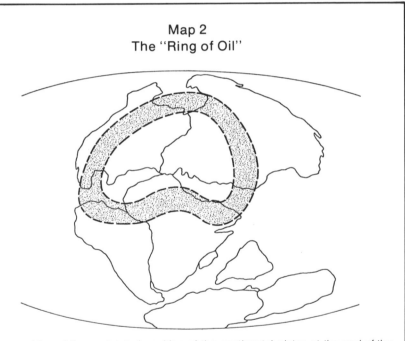

**Map 2
The "Ring of Oil"**

Source: Map of the postulated position of the continental plates at the end of the Triassic Period (180 million years ago), adapted from R. S. Dietz and J. C. Holden, "The Breakup of Pangea," *Scientific American*, Vol. 223, No. 5, November 1970, p. 35, and published in Richard Nehring, *Giant Oil Fields and World Oil Resources*, prepared for the Central Intelligence Agency (Santa Monica, Calif.: The Rand Corporation, 1978), p. 40.

[53]John R. Brodman and Richard E. Hamilton, *A Comparison of Energy Projections to 1985* (Paris: International Energy Agency, Organization for Economic Cooperation and Development, January 1979), p. 12.

5. The Soviet Union and Energy

For much of the twentieth century, Russia has exported oil. In the early 1970s, the Soviet Union held third place, behind the United States and Saudi Arabia, as a leading world oil producer. While Soviet oil exports between the two world wars went principally to Western Europe, in the early post-World War II period there was considerable resistance in the Western world to Soviet oil because of fears of becoming dependent on a strategically important commodity that in a crisis might be embargoed by Moscow. As a result, the Soviet Union found markets for its oil exports principally in less developed countries, where it often concluded barter deals, and in Eastern Europe, where the Soviet government offered preferential sales terms.

By the late 1950s, with the Suez crisis of 1956 and the temporary closing of the Suez Canal through which most oil destined for Europe then passed, there was growing interest in Soviet oil, especially in the case of Italy. In the 1960s, Italy ranked as the largest market for Soviet oil exports, exceeding any East European country.[54] By the early 1970s, all West European countries were importing some Soviet oil.

However, by the early 1970s, Soviet domestic consumption of oil and natural gas had risen substantially with the growth of the Soviet economy and a declining relative dependence on coal. Even by the late 1960s, the Soviet Union had become less willing than previously to supply East European communist states with raw materials at preferential prices, and had begun to urge the East European states to find other suppliers, including oil from the Middle East. Increasingly, the East European states have turned to non-Soviet sources for raw material imports, especially in the Middle East for oil. If this trend is accelerated in the next decade, both the Soviet Union and its East European allies will probably turn to the same sources as Western Europe, Japan and the United States for oil imports.

If the assessment is accurate, the problem facing consumer states arising from oil as an energy source will grow even further in the 1985-2000 time frame. In energy supply-demand relationships, the principal factor working in favor of consumer states in that longer time frame, as distinct from the 1980-1985 period, will be time itself—time to make the necessary investment in alternative energy sources to reduce anticipated shortfalls in supply. Because of lead-time factors, only after 1985—perhaps by the

---

[54]Marshall I. Goldman, "The Soviet Union," in Vernon, editor, *op. cit.*, p. 130.

1990s—will such alternative energy sources as coal, shale oil, oil from the sands, and the use of nuclear power on a far more substantial scale (to be discussed in a subsequent section) erode significantly the relative importance of petroleum for world energy needs.[55]

TABLE 3
Soviet Bloc: Oil and Natural Gas[1]

	Oil (million tons)[2]			Natural Gas (billion cu m)[3]		
USSR:	*1976*	*1980*	*1990*	*1976*	*1980*	*1990*
Production	520.0	640	780	320.0	430	750
Imports[3]	7.2	10	15	11.8	12	20
Exports[3]						
to East Europe	68.4	90	90	13.4	30	65
to West Europe	61.9	70	30	12.4	22	55
to other areas	18.2	20	25	—	—	—
Total	148.5	180	145	25.8	52	120
Apparent Consumption	378.7	470	650	306.0	390	650
Others:						
Production	17.8	20	20	54.0	50	55
Imports						
from USSR	68.4	90	90	13.4	30	65
from other areas	12.0	20	90	—	—	—
Total	80.4	110	180	13.4	30	65
Apparent Consumption	98.2	130	200	67.4	80	120
Total Area:						
Production	537.8	660	800	374.0	480	805
Net exports (-) or imports (+)	(-60.9)	(-60)	+50	(-0.6)	(-10)	(-35)
Apparent Consumption	476.9	600	850	373.4	470	770

[1]The area includes the USSR and the other full Comecon members in Eastern Europe, i.e., East Germany, Poland, Czechoslovakia, Hungary, Romania and Bulgaria. Actual figures are shown for 1976, forecasts for 1980 and 1990.

[2]Production of crude; imports/exports of crude and products.

[3]USSR import/export figures exclude Iranian deliveries, which are compensated under special arrangements by Russian deliveries to West Europe.

Source: Economic Commission for Europe: see B. A. Rahmer, "Soviet Union: Export Potential in Decline," *Petroleum Economist*, June 1978, p. 246.

[55]See *Geopolitics of Energy, op. cit.*, p. 26.

The question of world oil demand and supply is further complicated, as already suggested, by consumption and production trends in the Soviet Union. Although the Soviet Union is estimated to contain vast deposits of oil and natural gas,[56] production from existing fields is declining relative to demand.[57] By the mid-1980s, the CIA study estimated, the Soviet Union may have been transformed from a net exporter to a net importer of oil;[58] or, as noted in the ECE study cited earlier, the Soviet Union will export

---

[56]According to one recent study, "Whilst it is reasonable to postulate that 1.6×10^{12} cubic meters of new (natural gas) reserves will be proven annually in 1975-85, given the immense size of the fields being discovered in the Siberian tundra, the assumption that huge volumes of gas will be extracted and—an even more formidable problem—evacuated to a point where it has a use, is of quite a different order, and in fact, the Russians themselves have shown, if only by their attempts to obtain U.S. and Japanese assistance in these areas, that they are not convinced of being able to carry out the necessary work within the kind of timescale they would choose. Fields in West Siberia are already being tapped and pipelines laid, to achieve the level of production increase in the next five years which has been planned for the past five. But to maintain an annual 10 percent growth rate beyond 1980 and throughout the next quinquennium would probably require the proving up and bringing in of East Siberian reserves as well, and on the whole that seems unlikely on any significant scale within 10 years." *Soviet Natural Gas to 1985* (London: The Economist Intelligence Unit Limited, 1975), p. 12.

[57]*The International Energy Situation: Outlook to 1985,* Central Intelligence Agency, April 1977; *Prospects for Soviet Oil Production,* Central Intelligence Agency, July 1977. For a critique of these studies, see *The Soviet Oil Situation: An Evaluation of CIA Analyses of Soviet Oil Production*, Staff Report of the Senate Select Committee on Intelligence, United States Senate, May 1978:

"The forecast that the Soviet Union contains both a worst case and a best case scenario, as well as a consideration of the 'possible effects of conservation and substitution (a 2.5 percent reduction in energy consumption) as well as the effect of falling production and the domestic economy and international trade.' There is no explanation of how the 2.5 percent was derived other than that it is a 'highly subjective estimate.' (p. 14.)

"This study reports that if all energy conservation is focused on oil consumption, then the Soviets could reduce oil production to 9.4 million barrels per day by 1985. If, at the same time, oil production is on the high side of the CIA estimate (10 million barrels per day), then the Soviets would have enough oil to cover domestic needs. If, on the other hand, conservation is less successful and production is at the lower end of the CIA estimate (8 million barrels per day), then the shortfall of oil would need to be imported or, more likely, additional and more stringent steps would be taken by Soviet officials to prevent such an outcome."

[58]The emergence of the Soviet Union as a major net importer of oil would cast doubt upon one of the fundamental premises of Lenin's theory of Imperialism, namely that capitalist states engage in a scramble for overseas resources and markets which ultimately produces war and the destruction of the international system of capitalist states. Instead, dependence upon overseas resources is a function of industrialization, consumption, and endowments of resources within national frontiers rather than the nature of the economic and political system. To carry this analysis one step further: The Soviet Union, as noted elsewhere in this study, probably cannot develop fully its own indigenous sources of energy without access to the drilling and other technologies of an advanced capitalist state, namely, the United States.

substantially less oil because of declining rates of domestic production. For the Soviet Union to remain self-sufficient in oil, or to increase substantially its production in light of growing domestic demand, it would have to develop new fields located for the most part in the Siberian region under climatic and other conditions requiring large-scale investment, including the use of some of the most advanced extraction technologies now available only in the West. The locational problems confronting the Soviet Union in exploiting oil resources are said to have given impetus to the strong emphasis being placed on atomic power.[59] In the early 1970s, the United States and Japan expressed interest in providing investment and technologies for the exploitation of untapped Soviet oil and natural gas resources. Many obstacles were encountered. They included severe Soviet restrictions on prospecting to determine amounts of oil and natural gas contained in Siberian reserves; the reluctance of the Japanese to contemplate such a joint venture with the Soviet Union without American participation; and the failure of the Trade Expansion Act of the Nixon-Ford Administrations, which foundered on the Jackson Amendment on Soviet emigration and without which adequate guarantees by the U.S. government of American investment in Siberia became impossible.

Even if a decision were to be made now to develop Soviet Siberian oil and natural gas, the lead-time would be such as to have little effect on Soviet demand for energy imports in the next decade. Therefore, we face the prospect that the Soviet Union and East European communist states, which have been themselves dependent on Soviet energy imports, will enter the world market. The interruption in Iranian oil exports has already led East European states to what has been described as a desperate search for alternative sources of oil and natural gas.[60] Before the political turmoil in Iran, Iran supplied the Soviet Union with natural gas, and the Soviet Union, in turn, shipped an equivalent supply of natural gas to East European countries. Hungary, Czechoslovakia and Yugoslavia had contracted with Iran to supply turn-key factories, arms and construction projects, respectively, in return for oil. The effect of major increases in oil import bills on East European economies may be profound indeed, and energy shortages have already adversely affected production levels and brought substantial increases in the retail prices of petroleum products

---

[59]Robert W. Campbell, "The Soviet Union," in Gerard J. Mangone, editor, *Energy Policies of the World: Indonesia, the North Sea Countries, the Soviet Union*, Volume II (New York: Elsevier, 1977), p. 248.
[60]David A. Andenman, "East Bloc Seeks New Oil Sources," *New York Times*, February 20, 1979.

in 1978-1979. To what extent, for example, will balance of payments problems, together with internationally induced inflation, result in substantially lower growth rates, with possible domestic political consequences destabilizing for communist regimes, with what implications for the Soviet propensity to use coercion, and with what effects in turn potentially on Western Europe and the Atlantic Alliance? Numerous such linkages among energy issues and security problems affecting the interests of the United States and its allies can be conceptualized.

Whatever the effects upon East European economies and political systems, and upon relations among communist states, the growing dependence of Warsaw Pact countries on oil imports from outside the communist world will coincide with increased, or at least continuing high levels of, dependence by the United States, Western Europe and Japan upon oil imports and, in particular, upon increasing imports from the Persian Gulf. It is beyond the scope of this study to examine in great detail the implications of the potential entry of the Soviet Union and other Warsaw Pact members into the Middle East oil supplier markets. It is likely that the Soviet Union will seek preferential access to Persian Gulf oil by assisting forces bent upon replacing remaining noncommunist governments with revolutionary regimes. There is evidence of Soviet complicity in the internal strife that has beset Iran.[61] The stakes inherent in a radical transformation in Iran that is anti-Western and anti-American are extremely high for the Soviet Union. To forgo exploitation of such an opportunity to sharpen the differences among the United States and its allies, and to weaken their economies, would represent a change of historic proportions in Moscow's conception of its global objectives. The problems of supply interruption for Eastern Europe and the Soviet Union itself are of minor importance in light of the potential afforded for longer-term gain. While the causes of the fall of the Shah and the political turmoil in Iran are numerous, Soviet policy has been calculated to fan the flames of anti-Americanism and to support forces bent upon violence and revolution.

Of perhaps even greater significance is the recent Soviet invasion of Afghanistan. It can be argued that Moscow, reading the energy handwriting on the wall, has decided not to wait until the USSR and its satellites are in extremis with respect to energy and that the Afghan adventure is but the opening move in a brutal, overt move to seize the all-important

---

[61]See, for example, Robert Moss, "The Campaign to Destabilize Iran," *Conflict Studies*, No. 101, November 1978.

Middle East fields, without waiting for the longer-term and more uncertain results which would attend a campaign of subversion throughout the region.

The options available to the Soviet Union may thus extend beyond the disruption of oil from the Persian Gulf, and its denial to energy import-dependent states. If the Soviet Union itself gains access to Persian Gulf oil, it will be in a position to dictate the terms under which energy will be supplied to the United States, Western Europe and Japan. Moscow could use such leverage as a powerful ploy in its diplomacy. For example, the Soviet Union could increase its pressure upon Western Europe for a Central European disarmament scheme with the Federal Republic of Germany—a long-held Soviet objective designed to weaken and ulti-mately dissolve the Atlantic Alliance in return for assured supplies of oil. The Soviet Union could use control of oil in an attempt to compel West European and Japanese acquiescence in Soviet policies—a form of "finlandization" or oil blackmail. The ability of the Soviet Union to use oil to neutralize Western Europe would have enormous implications for Mos-cow's relations with Peking. It would increase greatly, to the advantage of the Soviet Union, the existing gap in military capabilities that already favors Moscow with respect to China. The Soviet Union would be able to concentrate its forces and attention upon China, either to bring about a resolution of the Sino-Soviet conflict favorable to Moscow's interests or to encircle China with growing Soviet military power in the Asian-Pacific region.

Soviet behavior in the period preceding, as well as during, the energy crisis of 1973-1974—a period when the Soviet Union itself did not have an oil supply problem—displayed three basic characteristics: (1) Mos-cow was eager to exacerbate tensions between oil producer and con-sumer states, to the extent of shipping arms on a massive scale to Arab client states and urging an increase in oil prices designed to weaken the industrialized consumer states. (2) The Kremlin sought to benefit eco-nomically from the crisis through the higher prices it could charge for oil exports from the Soviet Union. Thus, the Soviet Union officially adhered to a policy of refusing to sell oil to "embargoed" countries, while at the same time shipping petroleum during the crisis to both the Netherlands and the United States.[62] (3) Even before the October War, the Soviet Union extended encouragement to producing states to raise the price of

---

[62]Goldman, "The Soviet Union," in Vernon, editor, op. cit., p. 138.

oil and expressed during the crisis its support of supply disruption to the United States and its industrialized allies.[63]

During the October War, moreover, the Soviet Union is reported to have placed on alert several divisions of airborne troops for deployment to the Middle East and to have called upon the United States, in a message to President Nixon on October 24, 1973, to join with the Soviet Union in sending military forces to ensure a cease-fire between Egypt and Israel.[64] The Soviet note indicated that, in the absence of U.S. cooperation, the Soviet Union was prepared to act unilaterally.

If the Soviet Union emerges by the mid-1980s as a net importer of energy, this will coincide with the attainment by Moscow of a position of unprecedented military power. Suffice it to say here that a projection of present trends in the U.S.-Soviet strategic-military relationship may enable the Soviet Union to place at risk most of the fixed-, land-based U.S. strategic forces by virtue of substantial increases in missile accuracy and a throwweight advantage of more than five-to-one. We will have no corresponding or equivalent capability to pose a counterforce threat to Soviet fixed-, land-based strategic systems. Soviet air defenses, its civil defense program, and its strategic-military capability designed to project Soviet political influence on an unprecedented scale, could underwrite Moscow's diplomacy either to deny needed energy imports to industrialized noncommunist states or to make such imports dependent upon Moscow's good will. Hence, the energy problems confronting the United States and its allies are set within a broader strategic context. In the early 1980s our capacity to threaten the Soviet Union credibly with our strategic-nuclear power will have diminished at a time when our capacity for local intervention will be inadequate. Each of these interrelated issues must be the object of concern and action.

---

[63]Foy D. Kohler, Leon Gouré and Mose L. Harvey, *The Soviet Union and the October 1973 Middle East War: Implications for Detente* (Coral Gables, Fla.: Center for Advanced International Studies, University of Miami, Monographs in International Affairs, 1974).

[64]See Elmo R. Zumwalt, Jr., "The Lessons for NATO of Recent Military Experience," *The Atlantic Community Quarterly*, Winter 1974-75, pp. 456-459. See, by the same author, *On Watch: A Memoir* (New York: Quadrangle, New York Times Book Company, 1976), esp. pp. 440-450.

6. Intra-Alliance Relations: The Nuclear Energy Debate

Nuclear energy, the principal alternative to fossil fuels for certain important energy needs over the next generation, itself holds potential for discord between the United States and its industrialized allies, and specifically for U.S. relations with West European states and Japan. Although nuclear power will not provide, across the board, a substitute for petroleum for the remainder of this century, a substantial portion of world energy needs, especially the generation of large amounts of electricity, could and perhaps must be met by this energy source. According to the Committee on Nuclear and Alternative Energy Systems (CONAES), in a study on U.S. energy alternatives to the year 2010, prepared under the auspices of the U.S. National Academies of Sciences and Engineering, the average cost of nuclear electricity is less than that generated by coal, a difference that can be expected to continue in the future.[65]

The European Community expects nuclear power to account for about 10 percent of its primary energy consumption in 1985, and this will rise to as high as 20-25 percent by the year 2000, with nuclear power stations producing between 50 and 75 percent of the electricity consumed by the European Community. These goals are dependent on the national nuclear energy programs of EC members, for which projections have often been revised downward in recent years, largely as a result of domestic opposition to nuclear energy as well as differences in policy among the United States, Western Europe and Japan because of U.S. opposition to the "plutonium economy" and apprehension about the disposal of radioactive wastes and nuclear reactor safety.

The paradox, if not the internal contradiction or logical inconsistency, of U.S. nuclear energy policy stems from, on the one hand, placing emphasis on energy shortage forecasts for the future while, on the other hand, restricting severely, or at least postponing in effect to the end of the century, the development of one of the most promising new sources of energy. The issue to which nuclear power, and specifically nuclear reactor technology, is central revolves upon the extent to which, and the time-frame within which, energy consumers must either find substitutes for oil or face critical shortages. Hence, remaining known reserves of oil must be conserved for those uses for which there are no known substitutes—until technology enables us to find such substitutes. Where substitutes are potentially available, they must be developed in sufficient

---

[65]Harvey Brooks and Jack M. Hollander, "United States Energy Alternatives to 2010 and Beyond: The CONAES Study," *Annual Review of Energy 1979*, p. 34.

quantity at the time when they will be critically needed. Viewed in the perspective of future energy shortages, then, it appears that nuclear power is indispensable as a substitute form of energy to fossil fuels, especially oil. Reactor technology offers the prospect of providing an additional major source of energy by the 1990s and the early decades of the 21st century in an era between the decline in petroleum reserves relative to energy needs and the emergence of new forms of abundant energy. The dilemma facing energy-consuming states is that the shortages that they confront relate specifically to oil and gas, while most of the promising new sources are most suitable for the generation of electricity. The implication is clear: The United States and other nations will have to reduce drastically their consumption of oil and gas by conservation and/or by finding synthetic fluid fuels. It is evident that they face simultaneously the need to find non-fluid fuel substitutes, such as nuclear power, wherever possible, for oil and gas.

Most industrialized states, including the Soviet Union, have undertaken programs of nuclear reactor development. Early in the post-World War II period, the United States embarked on efforts to utilize the atom as an energy source, although by 1978 the United States was generating only 13 percent of its electricity from nuclear energy—far below what would have been technologically feasible,[66] but nevertheless equivalent to 1.4 million barrels of oil a day. Britain and France built nuclear reactors for the generation of electrical power, the former having participated in the wartime Manhattan Project. Both the British and French reactor programs, based on the gas graphite reactor design, had as a principal objective the production of plutonium for atomic weapons. Research on nuclear power for nonmilitary purposes was initiated in the Federal Republic of Germany in 1954, and in 1957 the European Community organization, Euratom, was founded as a means, albeit unsuccessful, to create a European atomic power industry.

The reasons for the failure of Euratom are numerous; they relate essentially to the priorities attached by its member states to national atomic energy programs in preference to a multilateral European effort. The refusal of France to share its gas graphite technology with Euratom partners led the Community to turn to the United States. Moreover, U.S. reactor technology offered more favorable prospects for Euratom than the gas

---

[66]In 1978 electricity accounted for 30 percent of the total energy needs of the United States. Of the electricity generated in the United States, 44 percent was produced from coal; 16 percent from oil; 13 percent from hydroelectric power; and 13 percent from nuclear power. See Peter Murray, "Nuclear Technologies: Existing and Potential," Paper presented at Conference on the Future of Nuclear Power, Honolulu, Hawaii, October 31-November 3, 1979, p. 9.

graphite programs of Britain and France.[67] But the first-generation national reactor programs of West European states, especially Britain[68] and France, were based upon the relatively unsophisticated technology of natural uranium, together with uncoordinated transnational engineering and marketing arrangements. The French hold the view, not without justification, that Euratom has provided principally a framework for the promotion of American light water reactor technology in Europe in preference to the gas graphite designs that France, as well as Britain, was producing. When France was unable to reorient the Euratom program toward gas graphite reactors, French policy toward Euratom became increasingly negative and hostile.[69] But France, too, eventually abandoned the gas graphite for the light water reactor, and pursued research on a new-generation reactor—the fast breeder.

The United States gained the technological lead with the development of the light water reactor that used enriched uranium. By the late 1960s all West European states, except Britain, had selected the American light water reactor in their nuclear energy programs. The United States was able to establish a dominant position in world export markets in the light water reactor, although other states such as Italy and Sweden, and including France, had begun to build light water reactors by 1975.[70] By the 1970s U.S.-designed reactors of this kind accounted for 85 percent of nuclear power in OECD countries. According to one analysis, U.S. governmental policy, under the "Atoms for Peace" program, encouraged the export of American light water nuclear reactors to Europe after the formation of Euratom in 1957. U.S. governmental policy in the 1950s precluded governmental subsidization of civil nuclear reactor development for fear that such assistance would put the government in the electric power business.

In effect, American nuclear policy during the 1950s promoted on one side of the Atlantic what it inhibited on the other. In Europe, American commercial interests benefitted from direct governmental financial support for the development of light

---

[67]Britain did not join Euratom until her accession to the Rome Treaties in January 1973.

[68]In April 1959, the United States and Euratom signed a Bilateral Agreement, under the terms of which Euratom received long-term assurance of an adequate supply of uranium at prices comparable to those for American industry; a guaranteed market for plutonium recovered from spent fuel; long-term capital loans for part of the cost of plant construction, and the reprocessing of spent fuel on terms to Euratom comparable to those offered in the United States.

[69]Henry R. Nau, *National Politics and International Technology: Nuclear Reactor Development in Western Europe* (Baltimore, Md.: The Johns Hopkins University Press, 1974), p. 127.

[70]OECD, *Uranium, Resources, Production and Demand* (Paris: OECD, 1975), p. 29. See also, De Carmoy, *op. cit.*

water reactors at a time when the Atomic Energy Commission's domestic reactor development policy inhibited such support at home.[71]

Westinghouse and General Electric, the two principal U.S. producers of light water reactors, were dominant in world markets outside the North Atlantic area, by virtue of direct exports or licensing agreements. Moreover, the United States provided the enriched uranium to nuclear reactors located in Europe and elsewhere. Thus, by the early 1970s, Western Europe and Japan had become dependent upon the United States for enriched uranium. In order to reduce their long-term dependence upon the United States, even before the 1973 energy crisis, the Europeans had begun to build their own enrichment plants in Europe, including two uranium enrichment consortia, Eurodif and Urenco, and to experiment with such techniques as the gas centrifuge and other systems.

One effect of the rapid rise in oil prices was to enhance for some countries the attractiveness of nuclear power, including the fast breeder reactor (FBR). Interest in the FBR reflects also a growing apprehension that by the end of the century uranium supplies will be drastically reduced, if not exhausted. Uranium must be regarded in itself as a scarce resource, to be utilized as efficiently as possible for the most important purposes. Therefore, the present generation reactors based on enrichment technologies themselves use a scarce resource, uranium, in which shortages could become apparent within the next decade even if additional reserves are discovered.[72] Unlike the United States, Western Europe and Japan are heavily dependent upon imports of natural uranium. The world's uranium reserves are located primarily in Australia, Canada, South Africa and the United States.[73]

Nuclear energy differs in one important respect from other non-renewable forms of energy because the size of the resource base depends on the type of nuclear fuel cycle that is used.

The present generation of light water reactors (LWRs) and their once-through fuel cycles utilize nuclear fuel very inefficiently, and are likely to exhaust the domestic supply of high-grade uranium in several decades. By contrast, if breeder reactors

---

[71] Irwin C. Bupp and Jean-Claude Derian, *Light Water: How the Nuclear Dream Dissolved* (New York: Basic Books, 1978), p. 36.

[72] *Geopolitics of Energy, op. cit.*, pp. 77-78.

[73] For a geological analysis of uranium availability, see Stanley Bowie, "Uranium and Its Future," *New Scientist*, July 20, 1978, p. 200. ". . . there is reasonable expectation that reserves could be developed to meet requirements to the early 1990s. But, if allowance is made for a forward reserve of 10 years, major new discoveries will be necessary. . . . The history of uranium discovery indicates an average addition of 65,150 tons of uranium per year over the past 33 years, which is much too low when compared with an estimated annual requirement of about 100,000 (tU) in ten years time and perhaps as much as

were to be developed and used, the domestic nuclear fuel supply could last for hundreds of thousands of years. An intermediate class of reactors and fuel cycles called advanced converters could under certain assumptions extend the domestic nuclear fuel supply for perhaps a century. Therefore, the future of nuclear energy in the United States will be determined by the timing and nature of follow-on developments and deployments to the present generation of LWRs.[74]

In contrast to earlier generation reactors, the fast breeder produces more fissionable materials than it uses, and is said to be potentially far more efficient in the production of energy. Hence, with the use of the breeder reactor on a substantial scale, scarce uranium reserves would be replenished, and the era of nuclear power extended by many years in meeting a portion of world energy needs. According to the Commission of the European Community, "Natural uranium sources are finite and supplies are by no means assured. . . . Reprocessing and fast breeders would make significant contributions to reducing dependence."[75] The European Community regards the breeder reactor as an "essential link in the Community strategy of reducing dependence on outside sources of energy." Therefore, in order to lessen the need for energy imports and to diversify energy sources, the European Community proposes to press the development of fast breeder reactors and the reprocessing of spent nuclear fuel—in both of which European and American policies are at odds. Nuclear fuel must be reprocessed periodically in the operation of breeder reactors. Therefore, the decisions taken by the U.S. government, beginning with the Ford Administration in October 1976 and continued by the Carter Administration, to suspend the reprocessing of uranium are consistent with the emerging American policy against the breeder reactor. Without reprocessing, there can be no plutonium either as fuel for breeder reactors or for plutonium-based nuclear weapons.[76] Here it may be argued that the prospects for nuclear weapons proliferation may be enhanced by the U.S. deferral of reprocessing and development of the breeder reactor. The greater the demand for oil imports by the United States, the greater the perceived need of other more energy-import dependent states to develop alternative sources such as the breeder.

200,000 (tU) by the end of the century." The author suggests that improved methods of detecting bigger deposits and more efficient mining methods could serve to augment world supplies. Nevertheless, he cautions that "the age and period over which uranium deposits formed emphasizes their irreplaceable nature, so far as man is concerned; also their geological characteristics and distribution clearly show their finite nature. Uranium is a rare element and should be used wisely."

[74]Brooks and Hollander, op. cit., p. 29.
[75]European Community Background Information, No. 22, July 29, 1977.
[76]See David J. Rose and Richard K. Lester, "Nuclear Power, Nuclear Weapons, and International Stability," Scientific American, April 1978, p. 46.

Because of the need for alternative energy sources, EC energy research programs place greatest emphasis on the early development of advanced nuclear fission technologies—specifically plutonium reprocessing/ recycling facilities and fast breeder reactors. By 1985-1990, it is assumed that the exploitation of plutonium technologies could reduce substantially the need for uranium imports (which account for over 80 percent of the total EC uranium supply);[77] and so long as current R&D programs are not delayed significantly, breeder reactors might in time (perhaps by 2025) virtually eliminate West European dependence on the uranium fuel cycle.[78] In any case, as FBRs produce more fissile material than they consume, a combined breeder/reprocessing capability would increase significantly the utilization of limited uranium supplies. For example, if an initial supply of about 5,000 tons of uranium (a level already in the hands of the EC states) were processed in FBRs, it is estimated that the energy produced would equal the estimated, technically recoverable reserves of North Sea oil (about 3 billion tons oil equivalent). If the EC's projected quota of reasonably assured world uranium reserves (some 1.2 million tons) underwent the same process, the energy produced would be sufficient to meet the energy needs of the EC countries, at their 1977 energy consumption rates, for more than 800 years.[79]

Since 1973, experimental and prototype breeder reactors have been operational in Western Europe. These include the French Phenix, with a 250 MWe capacity, the British PFR and the West German KNK. Several West European collaborative advanced reactor projects have also been initiated. With the Benelux countries, the German Federal Republic is developing a 200 MWe SNR reactor, scheduled for completion in 1982. In the early 1980s, France, Italy, Belgium, Holland and the Federal Republic plan to have an industrial version of the Phenix, known as the Super-Phenix, ready for operation. In addition, France and West Germany are engaged in collaboration on advanced reactors with respect to design standardization and joint marketing. Thus, there is growing interest in Western Europe in technological collaboration in the development, production and eventual sale of fast breeder reactors.

---

[77]In theory, reprocessing/recycling could cut Community uranium supply requirements by 30 percent per year, and enrichment workloads by some 15 percent per year. The need to build a plutonium stockpile for the initial fueling of FBRs, however, might cut these savings percentages in half. See *Points for a Community Strategy on the Reprocessing of Irradiated Nuclear Fuel* (Brussels: European Community Commission, July 2, 1977), p. 3.

[78]See *The Fast Breeder Option in the Community Context—Justification, Achievements, Problems and Action Perspectives* (Brussels: European Community Commission, July 28, 1977), p. 6.

[79]*Loc. cit.*

7. The United States and Nuclear Energy: Effects on Alliance Relations

Differences between the United States and its industrialized allies on nuclear energy antedated the Carter Administration. In fact, every U.S. Administration since 1945 has placed severe restrictions on the export of nuclear technology in order to diminish the prospects for nuclear weapons proliferation. But American policy since President Eisenhower's "Atoms for Peace" speech to the United Nations in December 1953 has also been governed by a perceived need to exploit nuclear energy "to serve the needs rather than the fears of mankind," under appropriate international safeguards and controls. For this purpose the International Atomic Energy Agency (IAEA) was created in 1955 under whose auspices a series of international safeguards was devised to reduce the likelihood that a nuclear program for peaceful purposes could become the means for producing an atomic weapons capability.[80] In addition, the United States pressed for the Non-Proliferation Treaty (NPT) which was concluded in 1968 to prohibit any state from assisting or encouraging a non-nuclear weapons state to acquire nuclear weapons. But the NPT, in keeping with the "Atoms for Peace" policy, gave ample scope to the peaceful uses of nuclear energy under appropriate international controls and safeguards. The 1960s, moreover, had been a period in which nuclear reactors were exported on a large scale, especially by the United States. Spent fuel was being reprocessed and plutonium extracted. Such activity seemed to fall clearly within the "Atoms for Peace" framework.

---

[80]The Safeguards Committee of the IAEA redefined safeguards in light of the Non-Proliferation Treaty in a document completed in 1971 setting forth the principles that should govern agreements between the Agency and national governments:

Article 28: The Agreement should provide that the objective of safeguards is the timely detection of diversion of significant quantities of nuclear material from peaceful nuclear activities to the manufacture of nuclear weapons or of other nuclear explosive devices or for purposes unknown, and deterrence of such diversion by the risk of early detection.

Article 29: To this end the Agreement should provide for the use of material accountancy as a safeguards measure of fundamental importance, with containment and surveillance as important complementary measures.

Article 30: The Agreement should provide that the technical conclusion of the Agency's verification activities shall be a statement in respect of each material balance area, of the amount of material unaccounted for over a specific period, giving the limits of accuracy of the amounts stated.

Quoted in C. Beets, "The Impact of International Safeguards Arrangements upon Nuclear-Fuel-Cycle Operation," in Abram Chayes and W. Bennett Lewis, editors, *International Arrangements for Nuclear Fuel Reprocessing* (Cambridge, Mass.: Ballinger, 1977), p. 80.

U.S. Restrictions on Highly Enriched Uranium, Plutonium and Fast Breeder Reactors

In the early 1970s several factors brought about a transformation in American policy that became manifest in the Presidential campaign of 1976 when both candidates called for new international restrictions on enriched uranium and plutonium separation. On October 29, 1976, President Ford, as noted earlier, suspended domestic U.S. reprocessing of enriched uranium and called for a three-year moratorium on the international transfer of enrichment or reprocessing technologies. The United States was prepared to give preference in supplying both civil reactors and nuclear fuels to states complying with U.S. efforts to restrict or defer nuclear reprocessing or enrichment. Thus, a new dimension was added to the meaning of nuclear proliferation from the American perspective. As Ian Smart has suggested: "Nuclear proliferation, which had been defined in the NPT as the acquisition of nuclear weapons by additional states, was henceforward to be interpreted in practice as including also the acquisition of the fissile raw material for weapons—highly enriched uranium or plutonium—or the ability to produce it."[81]

Whether this represents a fundamental change in American policy is debatable. Since the detonation of the first atomic device, the United States has sought to prevent the proliferation of nuclear weapons technologies. By the mid-1970s, the peaceful uses of nuclear energy—the possibility of breeder reactor technology, the plutonium economy—had begun to pose a threat to the other basic element of American policy—the ongoing effort to restrict the spread of nuclear weapons. The latter was considered to have priority over the former.

In the early 1970s there had been a substantial growth of interest in several industrialized non-nuclear weapons states—Japan, Sweden, the Netherlands, Italy and the Federal Republic of Germany—in uranium enrichment, together with the detonation by India of a "peaceful nuclear device" in May 1974 as a result of plutonium extracted from technologies provided by Canada for civil use. By the mid-1970s, however, the United States had objected strenuously to proposed German and French nuclear reactor and full nuclear fuel cycle technology sales to Third World states—especially the West German-Brazil agreement of 1975. In October 1976, President Ford had placed new restrictions on the sale of reprocessed nuclear fuel.

But the Carter Administration, in its policies with respect to nuclear energy and nuclear proliferation—which it viewed as inextricably

---

[81]Ian Smart, "Janus: The Nuclear God," *The World Today*, April 1978, p. 122.

linked—sharpened the issues that had divided the United States and its industrialized allies on nuclear power as a source of energy in the late twentieth century. Setting forth his nuclear policy at a press conference on April 7, 1977, President Carter declared that a "serious risk accompanies world-wide use of nuclear power" and that this risk "would be vastly increased by the further spread of sensitive technologies which entail direct access to plutonium, highly enriched uranium or other weapons useable material."[82] Thus, the Carter Administration evolved a nuclear energy policy providing for:

(1) Indefinite postponement of the commercial reprocessing and recycling of plutonium produced in the nuclear programs of the United States.

(2) Deferral of the date when fast breeder reactors would be put into commercial use in the United States, with priority to be given to research for alternative reactor designs and fuel cycles without direct access to materials useable in nuclear weapons. On November 5, 1977, the Carter Administration announced that the Clinch River, Tennessee, breeder reactor development project would be canceled.

(3) Continuation of an embargo on the export of technologies to promote uranium enrichment and commercial reprocessing.

(4) Broadening of discussions with both nuclear suppliers and recipients concerning approaches designed to reconcile the energy objectives of other states with the need to reduce the proliferation of nuclear weapons. Specifically, the United States proposed an international fuel cycle evaluation program to consider alternative fuel cycles and other measures to assure access to nuclear fuel supplies and spent fuel storage.

The Carter Administration's policy on the breeder reactor is based on the assumption not only that the potential risks of proliferation outweigh the potential gains in energy development, but also that uranium supplies are likely to be abundant at least until the early 21st century. On this issue, the official European Community and American positions diverge.[83] Here again, the United States, self-sufficient in uranium, enjoys

---

[82]*New York Times*, April 8, 1977.

[83]As in many of its other dimensions, the Carter Administration's energy policy on this aspect of nuclear power corresponds to the findings of the Ford Foundation Study, *Nuclear Power Issues and Choices* (Cambridge, Mass.: Ballinger, 1977). According to the Ford Foundation report, (p. 335), "There is not an impending absolute shortage of energy necessitating early breeder introduction. Breeders should therefore be evaluated on their economic and social merits relative to other present and future energy technologies. . . . The decision on commercialization of the breeder . . . can safely be postponed beyond the end of this century." Among the authors of the Ford Foundation study was Joseph Nye of Harvard University. Nye became Deputy to the Under Secretary for Security Assistance, Department of State, a position with principal responsibility for U.S. nuclear energy and weapons proliferation policies. Another author of the Ford Foundation study was Harold Brown, prior to his becoming Secretary of Defense.

an advantage not available to Western Europe, which contains no indigenous uranium supplies. In a period of constricting uranium availability,
the United States, it is feared, could place additional restrictions on
exports to Western Europe and Japan.

In announcing his decision to suspend fast breeder reactor development
in the United States, Carter called upon other industrial powers to take
similar action. In part, American opposition to European nuclear energy
policy was directed in the case of Carter, as it had been in the Ford
Administration, against the sale of reprocessing plants and technologies
by France and Germany, respectively, to Pakistan and Brazil, neither of
which are signatories of the Non-Proliferation Treaty.

In discussions at the London Summit Conference in May 1977, Carter,
together with Prime Minister Callaghan, Chancellor Schmidt, and President Giscard D'Estaing, agreed to establish the International Fuel Cycle
Evaluation (INFCE) Program. Its purpose was to devise, on a multilateral
basis over a two-year period, improved fuel cycle technologies with
reduced potential for nuclear weapons proliferation. The United States
pledged that it would maintain without changes its then existing uranium
supply arrangements until the completion of a two-year study on fuel
cycle technologies under the auspices of INFCE.

Although the study envisaged under INFCE was initiated in October 1977,
in February 1978 the United States Congress passed, and President
Carter placed his signature on, the Nuclear Non-Proliferation Act of 1978.
From the U.S. perspective, this Act was designed to achieve one of the
principal objectives of the Carter Administration: to tighten controls on
the use by other states of uranium supplied by the United States. The Act
had its most restrictive effects on allies of the United States—the most
advanced industrialized states with major nuclear power programs for
uranium enrichment, spent fuel reprocessing, and fast breeder development. The Act stipulated that contracts for the supply of U.S. uranium,
for example, to the European Community, some of which extended for
periods up to 1995, would have to be renegotiated.[84] The EC was given
a thirty-day deadline to renegotiate such contracts.

---

[84]The Act stipulates that all new Agreements for nuclear exports from the United States, in
keeping with past practice, must be submitted for approval to Congress, which retains
the power of veto by majority vote in both Houses within a 60-day period. However, all
existing agreements must be renegotiated to conform to criteria for new agreements.
These include prohibitions against the use of nuclear exports for explosive devices;
prohibition of further enrichment or transfer to third country, reprocessing of nuclear fuels
acquired from the United States without U.S. approval. See Frederick Williams, "The
United States Congress and Nonproliferation," *International Security*, Fall 1978, esp. pp.
45-47.

The Impact of U.S. Policy on Alliance Relationships

Aside from the abrupt alteration of the existing uranium supply agreements, the Act represented, from European[85] and Japanese perspectives,[86] a peremptory, unilateral, and abrupt change of U.S. policy. It bore resemblance to earlier times in relations between the United States and its allies, when important decisions were taken without adequate consultation—or in some cases, as in this, in the absence of any prior discussion with allies. To compound insult with injury, the U.S. legislation represented, from the perspective of allies, a breach of the agreement reached at the London summit conference concerning the U.S. supply of uranium during the two-year INFCE study.

INFCE created a framework for examination of the complex problems of reconciling, on the one hand, international security and nonproliferation with, on the other, nuclear power and energy security. Industrialized and less developed states were able to consider the problems posed by nuclear energy technologies for the proliferation of nuclear weapons in light of their energy needs in the years ahead. Although INFCE has diffused, temporarily at least, the growing opposition to U.S. nonproliferation policy as it relates to nuclear energy, it has not resulted in the reconciliation of diverse national perspectives in a commonly acceptable strategy. Because a fully proliferation-safe nuclear fuel cycle does not exist, it is not possible to devise a "technical" solution to the problem of reconciling nuclear energy and international security. Hence, INFCE does not endorse a particular fuel cycle or resolve the basic issues dividing the United States and other participants in the evaluation.[87]

Central to the Non-Proliferation Act of 1978 is the reprocessing of spent fuel from nuclear power reactors.[88] As noted earlier, reprocessing is indispensable to the breeder reactor. The U.S. legislation gives to the

---

[85]See Gunter Hildenbrand, "A German Reaction to U.S. Nonproliferation Policy," *ibid.*, p. 55. "Confidence in the United States as a leader into the nuclear energy age and as a reliable supplier of nuclear fuel has been shaken, and this mistrust is also being transferred to other exporting countries. The way in which present policy, as expressed in the NNPA 1978, sees fit to work toward non-proliferation by interfering in existing bilateral agreements and in relations between the United States and its customers and the countries they supply in turn, is not the best way to remove this mistrust."

[86]See, for example, Ryukicki Imai, "A Japanese Reaction to U.S. Nonproliferation Policy," *ibid.*, p. 64. According to Ryukicki Imai: "Keeping open as many sensible options as possible seems to be the favored approach to making policy in this age of uncertainty. To be deprived of this right through outside pressure is often regarded as a most serious challenge to national sovereignty. The notion of foreclosing those options involving a plutonium economy in favor of hypothetical scenarios based on the use of the year 2020 of fusion power or solar power is simply unacceptable."

[87]For a recent survey of this issue, see Chayes and Lewis, editors, *op. cit.*

[88]Williams, *op. cit.*, pp. 47-48.

United States a large measure of control over reprocessing activities and third-party transfers of nuclear fuels by U.S. allies in Western Europe and Japan. In particular, Britain and France are developing reprocessing facilities at Windscale and La Hague. Any fuel reprocessed in these installations that is of American origin, such as the 1977 French-Japanese agreement for the reprocessing of 1,600 tons of Japanese nuclear fuel at La Hague in the mid-1980s, would be subject to American approval. As Frederick Williams has suggested,

The added imposition of Criterion 6 (the prohibition of reprocessing without U.S. approval) on Euratom through export licenses and a renegotiated agreement for cooperation will give the U.S. a virtual veto power over commercial operations at Windscale and La Hague for years to come, since the fraction of nuclear fuel in use in Euratom and elsewhere which is of U.S. origin will remain for some time even if there are strenuous efforts to reduce dependence.[89]

As might have been anticipated, the least willing of West European states to comply with American requirements set forth in the Nuclear Non-Proliferation Act of 1978 was France. With its relatively large stocks of uranium and an indigenous enrichment capacity, France saw no need to acquiesce in U.S. pressure. The FRG and the remaining EC members expressed a willingness to meet the U.S. deadline for renegotiating existing agreements in order to retain access to U.S. enriched uranium supplies.

The legislation is especially onerous to the FRG because it would restrict the sale of technologies for reprocessing and enrichment without U.S. approval—and Bonn has been heavily dependent on U.S. nuclear technology and enriched uranium. The United States provides more than 60 percent of the low enriched uranium used in the FRG's commercial light water reactors and all of the highly enriched fuel for research reactors. The Soviet Union is the other principal supplier of low enriched uranium to the FRG.[90] In May 1978, the FRG, France and the United States agreed that the EC would enter negotiations with the United States on Euratom contracts, provided the issues being considered by INFCE were not included until its study was completed.

The issue of reprocessing nuclear fuel divides the United States and its principal allies, with Britain and France now developing their reprocessing plants at Windscale and La Hague. Such plants will reprocess spent fuel from nuclear reactors in other countries. The Carter Administration

[89]Pierre Lellouche, "International Nuclear Politics," *Foreign Affairs*, Winter 1979/1980, pp. 338-339.
[90]David Dangelmayer, "West Germany's Nuclear Dilemma," *New Scientist*, July 13, 1978, p. 104.

sought, without success, to have Britain and France defer construction of such plants until more effective controls for reprocessed nuclear fuels can be devised.

The United States, Britain and France are in accord that reprocessing facilities should not be located in non-nuclear weapons states. But the British and French position is that the provision of reprocessing services may, in fact, retard nuclear weapons proliferation by removing an incentive for non-nuclear weapons countries to acquire their own facilities for that purpose. To fail to offer such services may be tantamount to encouraging nuclear weapons proliferation.

This difference in approach pitted the British and French against the United States, since they have signed nuclear reprocessing contracts even since passage of the Nuclear Non-Proliferation Act of 1978. If Britain and France proceed with the reprocessing of nuclear fuels, they may run afoul of U.S. legislation as it applies to nuclear fuels provided by the United States. The result was to create a dilemma for the United States:

. . . strict consistency with its stated policy against premature reprocessing meant withholding assent to the transfer of spent fuel (arising from US-shipped fuel and reactors) to the European plants, thereby pulling the rug from under those allies and friends. But total acquiescence in the fulfillment of the contracts implied acceptance of defeat in the effort to control reprocessing and the widespread use of plutonium before adequate protection is in place.[91]

The Future of Nuclear Energy in the United States

In the early 1970s, and especially in the immediate aftermath of the October 1973 War and the energy crisis that ensued, the United States and its industrialized allies placed high hopes in nuclear power as an alternative to fossil fuels. In Project Independence, the Nixon Administration envisaged the use of nuclear power as the source of between 30 and 40 percent of U.S. electricity by the end of the 1980s and for as much as one-half by the start of the twenty-first century. Similarly optimistic assessments were made in other industrialized, energy import-dependent states. By the end of 1978 the United States had in operation 71 nuclear power plants, with about 90 additional plants either under construction or in possession of the necessary permits. There were an additional 40 plants on order. According to I. C. Bupp, even if all of these plants were to be built on schedule, the operating nuclear capacity available to the United States in the early 1990s would be about one-half of what had been officially projected in 1973.[92]

---

[91]Victor Gilinsky, "Plutonium, Proliferation, and the Price of Reprocessing," *Foreign Affairs*, Winter 1978-1979, p. 375.
[92]I. C. Bupp, "The Nuclear Stalemate," in Stobaugh and Yergin, editors, *op. cit.*, p. 111.

As a result of both the Three Mile Island accident and increasingly vocal opposition, the increase in nuclear power is likely to be far less dramatic. Whether there will be electricity shortages in the next decade will depend on the rate of growth in electricity demand and the extent to which generating plants—nuclear and non-nuclear—scheduled for completion will enter into service when expected. Because of the complex licensing procedures and lead-times in their development and construction, it is unlikely that new orders placed for nuclear power plants could have a major impact on energy sources before the 1990s. Yet the nuclear plants under construction at the time of the Three Mile Island accident, but whose completion may now be delayed or canceled, represent the potential equivalent of about 2 million barrels of oil a day in new supplies of energy. Moreover, existing plants may face the prospect of closure if a satisfactory system for nuclear disposal is not found in the years just ahead.[93] In short, by a combination of policies and as a result of uncertainties, we have effectively lost at least several years in the development of nuclear power as an alternative energy source.[94]

The promise of nuclear power inherent in the "Atoms for Peace" era between 1953 and 1973 has given way to uncertainty about the future of nuclear energy in the remaining years of the twentieth century. If the immediate effect of the quadrupling of oil prices, so it seemed, was to enhance the potential competitiveness of nuclear energy, the perceived difficulties inherent in nuclear power—its possible effects on weapons proliferation, together with problems of nuclear waste disposal, transportation of radioactive materials, nuclear reactor safety, and other environmental effects—cast doubt on its future, especially in the United States.[95] As one survey stated at the end of 1978:

---

[93]See *ibid.*, pp. 134-135.

[94]"Nuclear energy production in IEA member countries in 1977 accounted for 112 Mtoe or 5.1 percent of indigenous production, a substantial 23 percent increase compared with 1976 production of 91 Mtoe (4.2 percent of production). This increase was somewhat tempered by the virtual halt in new orders for nuclear powered reactions during 1977/78. Member countries now expect that nuclear energy will amount to 3lt Mtoe (11.1 percent of production) in 1985 and 547 Mtoe (17.2 percent of production) in 1990. These latest figures reflect the continued downward revision of expected nuclear contributions experienced since 1975. Major reasons for the lower nuclear projections include the following: lower electricity growth rates; continued concern about siting, safety, waste management and nonproliferation issues; increased cost of reactors and higher financing costs due to delays in construction. A general atmosphere of uncertainty now prevails compounded by instances of regulatory inconsistency or indecisiveness." *Energy Policies and Programmes of IEA Countries: 1978 Review* (Paris: Organization for Economic Cooperation and Development, 1979), pp. 25-26.

[95]Several states, including California, Iowa and Wisconsin, have prohibited further reactor construction until the nuclear waste issue is resolved. The state of Hawaii has mandated approval by the state legislature of the construction of nuclear reactors.

One by one, the lights are going out for the U.S. nuclear power industry. Reactor orders have plummeted from a high of 41 to zero this year (1978). Nuclear power stations are taking longer to build, and the delays are tacking hundreds of millions of dollars onto their costs. Waste disposal, which was supposed to be solved by now, is not. The export market is already glutted and shrinking fast. And the cumulative effect of these and other troubles has been a severe erosion of both public and political support for nuclear power.[96]

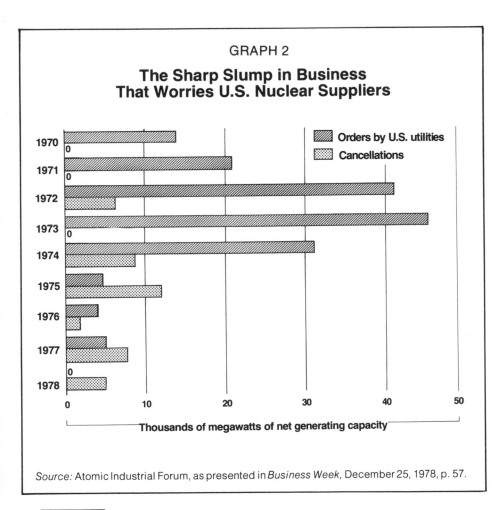

GRAPH 2

**The Sharp Slump in Business
That Worries U.S. Nuclear Suppliers**

Orders by U.S. utilities
Cancellations

Thousands of megawatts of net generating capacity

Source: Atomic Industrial Forum, as presented in *Business Week,* December 25, 1978, p. 57.

[96]"Nuclear Dilemma: The Atom's Fizzle in an Energy-Short World," *Business Week*, December 25, 1978, p. 54. For an in-depth analysis of the nuclear waste disposal and storage problem, see David A. Deese, *Nuclear Power and Radioactive Waste: A Sub-Seabed Disposal Option?* (Lexington, Mass: D. C. Heath, Lexington Books, 1978).

In the aftermath of the rapid increase in energy prices following the October War, electrical utilities in the United States revised downward to 4 percent their projections of demand growth which, until 1973, was increasing at an annual rate of 8 percent. Between 1970 and 1974, as a result, American electrical utilities had placed orders for 104 nuclear power plants. Graph 2 sets forth the dramatic decline in reactor orders in the United States since 1973. Here, again, the linkage between economic growth and the incentive for alternative energy sources noted earlier is illustrated by the decline in nuclear power construction as utility companies have reassessed their growth projections for the 1980s. Rising energy prices are likely to result in diminished demand in the absence of economic growth adequate to sustain new investment in alternative energy sources.

Since 1974, moreover, the U.S. electrical power generating industry has faced rapidly escalating costs for fuel, together with excess capacity, delays resulting from the organized protests and legal action by opponents of nuclear power, and increasing resistance imposed by the Environmental Protection Agency and other governmental groups. The controversial Seabrooke nuclear power project of the Public Service Company of New Hampshire is a case in point. Since 1971, when it was initiated, the project for a 2,000-megawatt twin reactor has become the focal point of environmentalists opposed to its construction on the New Hampshire coast, which is only 17 miles in length and, hence, it is argued, should be preserved in its entirety. The project has also encountered increasing opposition from legislative and consumer critics because of boosts in electricity rates to finance it. The cumulative effect of delays in the construction of Seabrooke has been to raise the price of construction from about $1 billion at the outset to more than $2.3 billion. As one analysis suggests, "the lesson of Seabrooke seems to be that for such a giant undertaking to pan out, everything has to go right and on schedule. For Public Service, almost nothing did."[97] In fact, the rate increase—amounting to about a 9 percent increase in a residential electric bill—approved by the New Hampshire Public Utilities Commission in May 1978 became a potent political issue similar to the "Proposition 13" tax reduction campaign in other states in the late 1970s and led to the defeat of incumbent Governor Meldrim Thomson. For a combination of reasons, the future of Seabrooke, like nuclear power itself, was in doubt in 1979. In light of the Seabrooke experience, along with the other problems facing the electric utility industry in the United States, orders for nuclear power facilities have been canceled or deferred.

[97]Donald D. Holt, "The Nuke that Became a Lethal Political Weapon," *Fortune*, January 15, 1979, p. 75.

8. Summary

The greater the discord within the United States and the divergence in policy between the United States, on the one hand, and Western Europe and Japan, on the other, on nuclear power issues, the greater the likelihood that they, individually and collectively, will fail to make maximum use of the potential offered by nuclear power as a source of energy needs. The more extensive the opposition to nuclear power at the official level in the United States, the greater the damage to pro-nuclear power forces in Western Europe and Japan, and the greater the perceived respectability of the coalition that, in most of the industrialized states, has mounted an increasingly formidable campaign against nuclear power. The opposition to nuclear power is based on a convergence of forces against nuclear weapons proliferation and against the effects of industrialization upon society—"arms controllers" and "environmentalists"— whose considerable strength was manifested in the nuclear power debate of the late 1970s. But it also includes those who retain doubts about nuclear power based on technical and economic uncertainties, even though there has been no systematic effort, especially in the United States, to evaluate the strengths and weaknesses, advantages and disadvantages, of nuclear power compared with other energy sources that will be available in the next generation. Such an evaluation, undertaken with objectivity, is necessary because the evidence is abundant that all sources of energy pose some risks, and have a variety of implications for man and his environment.

The numerous and complex problems of developing the technologies needed for the nuclear fuel cycle—including R&D lead-times of many years, investment, nuclear waste disposal, location of nuclear installations, reprocessing and enrichment, to mention only the most obvious— would be fraught with considerable potential for error and thus for controversy in the best of circumstances. Under prevailing conditions of discord, both within the United States and on a broader international scale, there will be less than optimum use of the time available to utilize nuclear power as effectively as possible as an energy source in the next generation. This, in turn, will help to perpetuate the dependence of the United States, Western Europe and Japan upon oil imports, with the potential for increasing competition for this scarce resource. Hence, there emerges a "linkage" or a relationship between national and alliance policies on nuclear power and oil. Competitive, conflicting, divergent approaches to alternative energy sources, especially nuclear power, enhance the likelihood that the problems facing consumer states with respect to oil will remain unsolved, and that tensions will even be exacerbated, depending on the economic projections and political trends outlined earlier.

In sum, the energy prospects for industrialized states in the 1980s, and perhaps in the remaining years of this century, have the following central elements:

(1) Economic factors alone may be sufficient to produce shortages, or at best a delicate balance between energy supply and demand. Even with the suspension of mandatory oil price controls in the United States, there is uncertainty about the future prospects for domestic oil providing a substitute for massive imports of petroleum.

(2) Political factors in the form of instability within Middle East oil-producing states, and perhaps on a broader level, will pose a grave danger to energy supply in the next decade. Hence, energy forecasts for the 1980s must give to political variables at least as much emphasis as economic factors have received in projections completed in the mid-to-late 1970s.

(3) The shorter the time available to find alternatives to Persian Gulf oil, the greater will be the need for the United States and its allies to consider the use of force in contingencies such as the harassment of tanker shipping, the closure of the Strait of Hormuz, and the disruption of oil production as a result of political instability in one or more oil-producing states. The establishment of bases in close proximity to the Persian Gulf—perhaps in Somalia, Egypt or Oman, together with the building of a rapid deployment force—becomes an urgent need for the United States. Closely related is the increased need to strengthen U.S. maritime forces in the Indian Ocean and to encourage a naval presence by other members of the Atlantic Alliance, especially France and Britain.

(4) By virtue of its growing military power, geographic proximity to the Persian Gulf and possible dependence on oil imports, the Soviet Union will play an increasingly active role in world energy issues of vital importance to the United States and its allies. This must prudently be assumed to be the motivation for a clearly evident Soviet drive for hegemony in the Persian Gulf region.

(5) At least for the next decade, oil will remain the world's most important source of energy. However, rapidly increasing oil prices will lead oil to be restricted to uses for which alternative forms of energy do not exist. Efforts must be made to discover and exploit new deposits of oil.

(6) No single alternative to oil exists and for a large number of uses there will be no adequate substitute in the next generation. Nevertheless, the development of nuclear power, taken together with other approaches to the energy problem, including conservation, would hold promise of having a substantial impact on energy supply over the next generation. Nuclear power represents one of several sources of energy that can and should be used in the next generation.

The emphasis in U.S. energy policy should be upon diversification of supply of existing sources and diversity in experimentation with new sources. In addition to nuclear fission, this includes controlled thermonuclear fusion, which has yet to be shown to be technologically feasible; but the prospect exists for major breakthroughs in controlled thermonuclear fusion in the remaining years of this century, thus providing the basis for a new source of energy in the 21st century. Other potential major sources for the next century include geothermal and solar energy, both of which will require extensive research.

(7) The evaluation of the extent to which nuclear power should form a source of energy must be undertaken in the context of a consideration of what resources will be available to the United States and other energy import-dependent states, together with their comparative advantages and disadvantages. In short, the benefits and costs of nuclear power should be examined in comparison with those of other energy sources.

INSTITUTE FOR FOREIGN POLICY ANALYSIS, INC.
List of Publications

Special Reports

THE CRUISE MISSILE: BARGAINING CHIP OR DEFENSE BARGAIN? By Robert L. Pfaltzgraff, Jr., and Jacquelyn K. Davis. January 1977. x, 53pp. $3.00.

EUROCOMMUNISM AND THE ATLANTIC ALLIANCE By James E. Dougherty and Diane K. Pfaltzgraff. January 1977. xiv, 66pp. $3.00.

THE NEUTRON BOMB: POLITICAL, TECHNOLOGICAL AND MILITARY ISSUES. By S. T. Cohen. November 1978. xii, 95pp. $6.50.

SALT II AND U.S.-SOVIET STRATEGIC FORCES. By Jacquelyn K. Davis, Patrick J. Friel and Robert L. Pfaltzgraff, Jr. June 1979. xii, 51pp. $5.00.

THE EMERGING STRATEGIC ENVIRONMENT: IMPLICATIONS FOR BALLISTIC MISSILE DEFENSE. By Leon Gouré, William G. Hyland and Colin S. Gray. December 1979. xi, 75pp. $6.50.

THE SOVIET UNION AND BALLISTIC MISSILE DEFENSE. By Jacquelyn K. Davis, Uri Ra'anan, Robert L. Pfaltzgraff, Jr., Michael J. Deane and John M. Collins. April 1980. 50pp. $6.50.

ENERGY ISSUES AND ALLIANCE RELATIONSHIPS: THE UNITED STATES, WESTERN EUROPE AND JAPAN. By Robert L. Pfaltzgraff, Jr. April 1980. xii, 72pp. $6.50.

U.S. STRATEGIC-NUCLEAR POLICY AND BALLISTIC MISSILE DEFENSE: THE 1980S AND BEYOND. By William S. Schneider, Jr., Donald G. Brennan, Hans Rühle and William A. Davis, Jr. May 1980. 61pp. $6.50.

Foreign Policy Reports

The papers in this series of Foreign Policy Reports are addressed to a variety of topics in the field of world affairs, including diplomacy, economics, strategy, science and technology, arms control, international organization, and country and regional issues.

DEFENSE TECHNOLOGY AND THE ATLANTIC ALLIANCE: COMPETITION OR COLLABORATION? By Frank T. J. Bray and Michael Moodie. April 1977. 42pp. $5.00.

IRAN'S QUEST FOR SECURITY: U.S. ARMS TRANSFERS AND THE NUCLEAR OPTION. By Alvin J. Cottrell and James E. Dougherty. May 1977. 59pp. $5.00.

ETHIOPIA, THE HORN OF AFRICA, AND U.S. POLICY. By John H. Spencer. September 1977. 69pp. $5.00.

BEYOND THE ARAB-ISRAELI SETTLEMENT: NEW DIRECTIONS FOR U.S. POLICY IN THE MIDDLE EAST. By R. K. Ramazani. September 1977. 69pp. $5.00.

SPAIN, THE MONARCHY AND THE ATLANTIC COMMUNITY. By David C. Jordan. June 1979. 55pp. $5.00.

Books

ATLANTIC COMMUNITY IN CRISIS: A REDEFINITION OF THE ATLANTIC RELATIONSHIP. Edited by Walter F. Hahn and Robert L. Pfaltzgraff, Jr. Pergamon Press, 1979. 386pp. $37.50.

SOVIET MILITARY STRATEGY IN EUROPE. By Joseph D. Douglass, Jr. Pergamon Press, 1980. 252pp. $30.00.